A CHRISTIAN MISCELLANY

Packed with useless (and useful) information about everything

   from the garden of Eden
                           to Armageddon,
  and from the five points
                of Calvinism
                         to the seven deadly sins.

Includes poetry, terrible jokes, useful facts, memorable quotes, vital creeds, eccentric lives, Bible typos and mistranslations, church ads, Bible howlers, and much more . . .

A
CHRISTIAN
MISCELLANY

*Terrible Jokes,
Curious Facts,
and Memorable Quotes
from the Garden of Eden
to Armageddon*

TIM DOWLEY

WILLIAM B. EERDMANS PUBLISHING COMPANY
GRAND RAPIDS, MICHIGAN

Wm. B. Eerdmans Publishing Co.
4035 Park East Court SE, Grand Rapids, Michigan 49546
www.eerdmans.com

© 2022 Tim Dowley
All rights reserved
Published 2022
Printed in the United States of America

28 27 26 25 24 23 22   1 2 3 4 5 6 7

ISBN 978-0-8028-7982-0

Library of Congress Cataloging-in-Publication Data

A catalog record for this book is available from the Library of Congress.

Unless noted otherwise, biblical quotations follow
the King James Version.

On Love 1 "St. Patrick's Breastplate" 2 Some Memorable Epitaphs 3 *Ave Maria* 4 On Death 4 Collect for Purity 5 Traditions of the Magi 5 The Cross 6 The Fundamentals 7 Art and Nature 7 "Trees" 7 Death Is Nothing at All 8 Gematria—Bible Math 9 "Doing Good" 10 Sermons 10 Where Was the Garden of Eden? 10 Wesley's Last Letter 11 "Ain't I a Woman?" 12 Angelology 13 The Ten Oldest Men in the Bible 13 Lost and Found 13 God's Peculiar People 14 The Shakespeare Psalm 15 Unsingable Hymns 16 Bible Animals 17 Spoonerisms 18 Noah's Ark Jokes 18 Great Opening Lines of Scripture 19 Mercy 20 Bible Names Best Not Given to Your Children 21 Peace in Our Time 21 How the Bible Was Divided Up 21 "The Lamb" 22 On Scripture 23 Careless Confirmation 24 A City on a Hill 24 The Ten Plagues of Egypt 25 The Beatitudes 25 How to Elect a Pope 26 Serenity 27 The Daily Office 28 Angels 28 The Shepherd Psalm 28 Some Bible Howlers 29 Atheist's Hymn 30 Banned! 31 Luther at the Diet of Worms 31 Popular Wedding Music 32 Hand and Eye 33 Corny Church Ads 33 Jesus's Final Week 34 An Easy Life? 35 Seasons 36 "I Am" 36 Ten Songs Referencing "Amazing Grace" 37 Biblical Bottles 37 John Wesley's Heart Warmed 38 Complaint 39 A Gathering of British Saints 39 Time's Paces 40 Bibliomancy 40 "Day by Day" 40 Some Bible Firsts 41 The Gate of the Year 41 The Right Hymn for the Job 42 "What Is Dying?" 42 The Apocrypha 43 Bible Giants 44 The Presbyterian Cat 44 Life on Earth 45 Peace 45 Ten Movies about Faith, Doubt, and Sin 46 Some Bible Misprints 47 Pursuit 48 Some Names and Descriptions of the Devil 49 Prayer of St. Francis 50 Charlemagne's Relics 50 "When Earth's Last Picture Is Painted" 51 Blessings 52 The Fate of the Apostles 53 A Grace 54 Some Religious Plays 54 "Temptation" 55 Why "the Bible"? 56 Anyone in the Quad? 56 "Proficiscere" 57 "The Bible Is an Antique Volume" 57 Biblical Records 58 On Marriage 59 John Wesley's Advice to Preachers 59 A Pilgrim's Prayer 60 Who Are the Gideons? 60 When Was the World Created? 61 The Shepherd 61 "The Donkey" 61 A Welsh Village Baptism 62 Parsons Peculiar 62 Darwin's Denial 63 On Slavery 64 Love and Truth 64 Does the Bible Really Say That? 65 Liturgy for Doubters 66 Hymn for the Last

Church of All 66 The Apostle Paul 66 Words of the Martyrs 66 For Whom the Bell Tolls 67 Essential Bible Manuscripts 67 On Understanding Scripture 68 Prophets 69 Stirring Last Words 69 Troubles 70 More Words on the Good Book 71 *Ave Maria Gratia Plena* 72 Adam and Eve 73 Some Scary Theological Terms 73 Scripture Unawares 74 "Pied Beauty" 74 The Apostles' Creed 75 Jesus's Seven Last Words from the Cross 75 "Love Divine" 76 One Solitary Life 77 Some Classics of Spirituality 78 The Pope Is Dead 78 The Four Evangelists and Their Symbols 78 Common Phrases from the Prayer Book 79 Anti-Semitism Challenged 80 Prayer of St. Columba 80 Names of God 80 Like Christ 81 *Jesus soit en ma teste* 81 Major Jewish Festivals 82 Finishing 83 Ten Sacred Music Masterworks 83 Faith and Works 84 Some Writers' Epitaphs 84 Ten Strong Things 85 Some Christian Classics 86 "Time Is" 86 Sojourners 87 Iconic Paintings 87 A Villain Passes 88 A New World 88 The Seven Penitential Psalms 89 More Corny Church Ads 89 You Call Me . . . 90 The Love Chapter 91 Hope 92 As the Bishop Said to the Actress 92 Who Were the Twelve Apostles? 93 Prayer of St. Ignatius 94 Some National Saints and Their Feast Days 94 Holy Moses . . . 96 Why Is It Called "the Mass"? 96 From "A Better Resurrection" 96 Denominations with Memorable Names 97 I Am 97 Was There a Bethlehem Stable? 98 How to Speak of God 98 "Teresa's Bookmark" 99 The Four Horsemen of the Apocalypse 99 Ichthus 100 Varieties of Monks 100 Bereavement 101 The Tribes of Israel 101 More Peculiar Parsons 102 Stations of the Cross (*Via Crucis* or *Via Dolorosa*) 102 "Love" 104 Titles for the Bible 104 The Septuagint and Vulgate 105 The Seven Deadly Sins and the Seven Virtues 105 The Tetragrammaton 106 Jacob's Pillow 107 The Seven Sorrows of the Virgin Mary 107 Who Wrote the King James Version? 108 Ten Terrifying Exorcism Movies 108 Does the Bible Really Say That? 109 How Many Crusades? 110 Some Titles for Jesus 111 Stigmatics 111 Millennialisms 112 Heaven 113 Clergy Dress 114 Humility 114 Seven Sacraments 115 More Bible Misprints 115 Unnamed 116 What a Way to Go 117 Five Points of Calvinism 117 Contentment 118 Some Scriptural Titles for the Holy Spirit 119 Adam's First Wife 119 "Remember" 119 Mr. Valiant-for-

Truth Passes Over 120 The Seven Churches of Revelation 121 Seven Ecumenical Councils 121 Witches and the Bible 122 Bibles Great and Small 122 Landmark Bible Movies 123 Legends of the Saints 125 Some Classic Hymns 126 When Is Easter? 127 Ten Major Discoveries in Biblical Archaeology 127 Nicknames for Bible Versions 129 "Lighten Our Darkness" 130 "For I Will Consider My Cat Jeoffry" 130 "Our Last Awakening" 132 "The Latest Decalogue" 132 Something Eternal 133 Fire 134 The General Confession 135 "In the Bleak Midwinter" 135 Gosse's Christmas 136 "Upon Christ His Birth" 137 "The First Blast of the Trumpet against the Monstrous Regiment of Women" 138 Chosen? 139 Westminster Shorter Catechism 140 Jesus's Parables in Matthew, Mark, and Luke 141 More Scripture Unawares 143 "E Tenebris" 143 Inkling Wisdom 144 Bad Popes 145 Sonnet 19 146 Monastic Orders 147 Some Fictional Lives of Jesus 148 "Crossing the Bar" 149 The Barebone Family 150 Terrible Religious Jokes 150 Churchy Words 151 Some Archbishops of Canterbury 152 A Long Wait 153 Luther on Relics 154 "Address to the Devil" 154 Patriotism Is Not Enough 154 Hypocrisy 155 Laughing in Church 155 Ten Facts about the Dead Sea Scrolls 156 Ten Novels about King David 157

ON LOVE

He who loves not lives not.

> *—Raymond Llull (c. 1232–c. 1315),*
> *mathematician and mystic*

There is nothing so difficult, and no stronghold so impregnable, that it cannot be broken down—and you built up—by love.

> *—Catherine of Siena (1347–1380),*
> *mystical author*

. . . love is oure lordes mening. And I saw fulle sekerly [with certainty] in this and in alle, that or [ere] God made us he loved us, which love was never sleked [lessened], ne never shalle. And in this love he hath done all his werkes, and in this love he hath made alle things profitable to us.

> *—Julian of Norwich (1343–c. 1416),*
> *mystical writer*

Love all God's creation, the whole and every grain of sand in it. Love every leaf, every ray of God's light. Love the animals, love the plants, love everything. If you love everything, you will perceive the divine mystery in things. Once you perceive it, you will begin to comprehend it better every day. And you will come at last to love the whole world with an all-embracing love.

> *—from* The Brothers Karamazov,
> *Fyodor Dostoyevsky (1821–1881), Russian novelist*

He said "Love . . . as I have loved you." We cannot love too much.

> *—Amy Carmichael (1867–1951), missionary*

The root of the matter (if we want a stable world) is a very simple and old-fashioned thing. . . . The thing I mean . . . is love, Christian love, or compassion. If you feel this, you have a motive for existence, a guide in action, a reason for courage, an imperative necessity for intellectual honesty.

—from The Impact of Science on Society,
Bertrand Russell (1872–1970), philosopher

Love is strong as death; but nothing else is as strong as either; and both, love and death, met in Christ. How strong and powerful upon you, then, should that instruction be, that comes to you from both these, the love and death of Jesus Christ!

—from Sermons,
John Donne (1572–1631), English writer

"ST. PATRICK'S BREASTPLATE"

I bind unto myself today
the power of God to hold and lead,
God's eye to watch, God's might to stay,
God's ear to hearken to my need,
the wisdom of my God to teach,
God's hand to guide, God's shield to ward,
the word of God to give me speech,
God's heavenly host to be my guard.

Christ be with me, Christ within me,
Christ behind me, Christ before me,
Christ beside me, Christ to win me,
Christ to comfort and restore me.
Christ beneath me, Christ above me,
Christ in quiet, Christ in danger,
Christ in hearts of all that love me,
Christ in mouth of friend and stranger.

*—extract from a version adapted as a hymn
by Cecil Frances Alexander (1818–1895). The original
is attributed to St. Patrick of Ireland (c. 390–460).*

SOME MEMORABLE EPITAPHS

Nature, and Nature's laws lay hid in night,
God said, *Let Newton be!* and all was light.

> —*by Alexander Pope (1688–1744),*
> *intended for Sir Isaac Newton (1643–1727)*

Response

It did not last: the Devil howling "Ho!
Let Einstein be!" restored the status quo.

> —*J. C. Squire (1884–1958)*

Here lies the body of Jonathan Swift, of this Cathedral Church, Dean, where savage indignation can no longer lacerate his heart. Traveller, go, imitate if you can his strenuous vindication of human liberty.

> —*Jonathan Swift (1667–1745), author of*
> Gulliver's Travels, *St. Patrick's Cathedral,*
> *Dublin; translated from the Latin*

Lector si monumentum requiris circumspice.
(Reader, if you seek his monument, look around you.)

> —*Sir Christopher Wren (1632–1723), St. Paul's*
> *Cathedral, London, of which he was the architect*

Here lyes HENRY PURCELL, Esqr. who left this life and is gone to that blessed place where only his harmony can be exceeded.

> —*Henry Purcell (1659–1695),*
> *Westminster Abbey, London, where he was organist*

Men must endure their going hence.

> —*C. S. Lewis (1898–1963), Holy Trinity Church,*
> *Headington Quarry, Oxford.*
> *From William Shakespeare:* King Lear, *act 5, scene 2*

Free at last, Free at last,
Thank God Almighty
I'm Free at last.

—Martin Luther King Jr. (1929–1968),
Atlanta, Georgia

AVE MARIA

Ave Maria, gratia plena,
Dominus tecum.
Benedicta tu in mulieribus,
et benedictus fructus ventris tui, Iesus.
Sancta Maria, Mater Dei,
ora pro nobis peccatoribus,
nunc et in hora mortis nostrae.
Amen.

Hail Mary, full of Grace,
the Lord is with thee.
Blessed art thou amongst women,
and blessed is the fruit of thy womb, Jesus.
Holy Mary, Mother of God,
pray for us sinners,
now and at the hour of death.
Amen.

—basis of the Roman Catholic Rosary and
Angelus prayers, incorporating two greetings
to Mary in Luke's Gospel (Luke 1:28, 42)

ON DEATH

Death, be not proud, though some have called thee
Mighty and dreadful, for thou art not so . . .

One short sleep past, we wake eternally
And death shall be no more; Death, thou shalt die.

> —*from "Death Be Not Proud,"*
> *John Donne (1572–1631), English writer*

Be near me, Lord, when dying,
O part not thou from me!
And to my succour flying,
Come, Lord, and set me free!
And when my heart must languish
In death's last awful throe,
Release me from mine anguish
By thine own pain and woe.

> —*from* St. Matthew Passion,
> *Johann Sebastian Bach (1685–1750), composer*

COLLECT FOR PURITY

Almighty God, unto whom all hearts are open, all desires known, and from whom no secrets are hid; cleanse the thoughts of our hearts by the inspiration of thy Holy Spirit, that we may perfectly love thee, and worthily magnify thy holy Name, through Jesus Christ our Lord.

> —*translation by Archbishop Thomas Cranmer*
> *(1489–1556) from the tenth-century Latin*
> Sacramentarium Fuldense

TRADITIONS OF THE MAGI

Numerous myths and legends have arisen around the "wise men" of Matthew 2. By tradition known as the "Magi," they are also referred to as "Three Wise Men" and "Three Kings," bringing gifts to the baby Jesus and alerting King Herod to his birth.

"Magi" is the plural of "magus," a member of a Persian priestly caste.

The Bible never names the Magi, nor does it say how many there were. Matthew's Gospel lists three gifts—gold, frankincense, and myrrh—so it's frequently assumed there were three Magi.

The Magi are often named as Caspar, Melchior, and Balthasar. Other names include Larvandad, Hormisdad, and Gushnasaph.

The Eastern Church claims there were twelve Magi.

Western Christian art depicts two, three, four—and as many as eight Magi.

The gifts of the Magi are interpreted symbolically: gold representing Christ's kingship; frankincense—the purest incense—his divinity; myrrh—a medicine—his humanity.

The Magi followed the Star of Bethlehem to find Jesus. Some believe this to have been a comet; others, a conjunction of the planets Jupiter and Saturn.

In the 1270s, the Venetian traveler Marco Polo claimed to have visited the tombs of the Magi: "In Persia is the city of Saba, from which the three Magi set out, and in this city they are buried, in three very large and beautiful monuments, side by side. . . . The bodies are still intact, with hair and beard remaining."

Cologne Cathedral, Germany, claims to preserve the bones of the Magi in the Shrine of the Three Kings.

THE CROSS

> The cross is the way of the lost.
> The cross is the staff of the lame.
> The cross is the guide of the blind.
> The cross is the strength of the weak.
> The cross is the hope of the hopeless.
> The cross is the freedom of slaves.
> The cross is the water of seeds.
> The cross is the cloth of the naked.
> The cross is the peace of the church.
>
> —*St. Yared (505–571), Ethiopian composer (adapted)*

THE FUNDAMENTALS

In 1895, at the Niagara Bible Conference, Ontario, Canada, a group of Christians listed what they defined as five "fundamentals of the faith"—from which the term "fundamentalism" arose. These fundamentals are often listed as

1. The inspiration and inerrancy of Scripture
2. The deity and virgin birth of Jesus Christ
3. Christ's substitutionary atonement on the cross for our sins
4. Christ's physical resurrection and personal bodily return
5. The authenticity of Christ's miracles

ART AND NATURE

> The world is a work of art, set before all for contemplation, so that through it the wisdom of him who created it should be known.
>
> *—from* Exegetical Works, On the Hexameron, *Basil of Caesarea (St. Basil the Great, 330–379), Orthodox theologian*

> True painting is only the image of the perfection of God, a shadow of the pencil with which he paints, a melody, a striving after harmony.
>
> *—Michelangelo Buonarroti (1475–1564), Italian artist*

> Painting is saying "Ta" to God.
>
> *—Stanley Spencer (1891–1959), English painter, quoted in a letter from Spencer's daughter Shirin to the* Observer, *February 7, 1988*

"TREES"

> I think that I shall never see
> A poem lovely as a tree.

A tree whose hungry mouth is prest
Against the sweet earth's flowing breast;

A tree that looks at God all day,
And lifts her leafy arms to pray;

A tree that may in summer wear
A nest of robins in her hair;

Upon whose bosom snow has lain;
Who intimately lives with rain.

Poems are made by fools like me,
But only God can make a tree.

> —*"Trees," Joyce Kilmer (1886–1918), American poet,*
> *killed fighting in World War I*

DEATH IS NOTHING AT ALL

Henry Scott-Holland (1847–1918), canon of St. Paul's Cathedral, delivered a memorable sermon on death entitled "The King of Terrors" on Whitsunday 1910, while the body of Edward VII was lying in state at Westminster. It includes this passage, written as if by the departed loved one:

> Death is nothing at all. It does not count. I have only slipped away into the next room. Nothing has happened. Everything remains exactly as it was. I am I, and you are you, and the old life that we lived so fondly together is untouched, unchanged. Whatever we were to each other, that we are still. Call me by the old familiar name. Speak to me in the easy way which you always used. Put no difference into your tone. Wear no forced air of solemnity or sorrow. Laugh as we always laughed at the little jokes that we enjoyed together. Play, smile, think of me,

pray for me. Let my name be ever the household word that it always was. Let it be spoken without an effort, without the ghost of a shadow upon it. Life means all that it ever meant. It is the same as it ever was. There is absolute and unbroken continuity. What is this death but a negligible accident? Why should I be out of mind because I am out of sight? I am but waiting for you, for an interval, somewhere very near, just round the corner. All is well. Nothing is hurt; nothing is lost. One brief moment and all will be as it was before. How we shall laugh at the trouble of parting when we meet again!

GEMATRIA—BIBLE MATH

Gematria is a method of interpreting Scripture by exploring the relationship between words and phrases with the same numerical value, after the values of their letters have been added together, or substituting one word or phrase for another of the same value.

In this scheme, each letter of the Hebrew alphabet is allocated a numerical value: for instance, aleph = 1, beth = 2, yod = 10, tav = 400.

As an example, in Genesis 28:12, Jacob dreams of a ladder to heaven. In gematria, the Hebrew word for "ladder" has a numerical value of 130—identical in numerical value to "Sinai." So, it is argued, the law revealed to Moses at Sinai is humankind's path/ladder to heaven.

In another example: "David" (dwd) has a value of 14, while in Matthew's Gospel Jesus's ancestors are listed in three groups of 14.

Gematria can also be applied to other languages. In English, the twenty-six letters of the alphabet are normally given the values 1 to 26—which results in the total 74 for both "Jesus" and "Messiah."

A notorious example of gematria is making 666—the "number of the beast" (Rev. 13:18)—refer to the Roman emperor Nero. If Greek letters for "Caesar Nero" are replaced with Hebrew letters, the result is *qsr nrwn*, which, given their numerical equivalents, add up to 666.

"DOING GOOD"

Do all the good you can,
By all the means you can,
In all the ways you can,
In all the places you can,
At all the times you can,
To all the people you can,
As long as ever you can.

—attributed—probably wrongly—to John Wesley
(1703-1791), English evangelist;
first known citation 1896

SERMONS

There is perhaps no greater hardship at present inflicted on mankind in civilized and free countries than the necessity of listening to sermons. No one but a preaching clergyman has, in these realms, the power of compelling an audience to sit silent and be tormented. No one but a preaching clergyman can revel in platitudes, truisms and untruisms, and yet receive, as his undisputed privilege, the same respectful demeanour as though words of impassioned eloquence, or persuasive logic, fell from his lips.

—from Barchester Towers,
Anthony Trollope (1815-1882)

WHERE WAS THE GARDEN OF EDEN?

Many locations have been proposed.

> *Southern Iraq*: Sumer, where the Euphrates and Tigris Rivers join. The Pishon and Gihon Rivers (see Gen. 2:8-14) are both long-since-disappeared tributaries of the Tigris and Euphrates.
> *Northern Iran*: The British archaeologist David Rohl (1950-) has claimed that Eden is a fertile valley in Iran, 120 miles

from Tabriz, and the biblical Gihon and Pishon are the rivers Araxes and Uizhun.

Israel: Some people believe Eden was in the Holy Land, and that the Jordan River flowed into the garden before dividing four ways.

Egypt: Some believe the Nile region alone fits the description of Eden in Genesis.

East Africa: Because the oldest human remains have been discovered in East Africa, some believe the garden of Eden to have been located there.

Java: In 1891, archaeologists found remains of Pithecanthropus (*Homo erectus*) in Java, which has therefore been suggested as the site of the garden of Eden.

Praslin Island, Seychelles: General Charles Gordon (1833-1885)—who also claimed (mistakenly) to have discovered the site of Golgotha—was convinced that this exotic island was the location of Eden, and that the rare coco de mer tree (Lodoicea)—found only here and on one other island in the Seychelles—was the tree of the knowledge of good and evil.

Galesville, Wisconsin: In 1886, Rev. D. O. Van Slyke (1818-1891) claimed that Eden was located between the Alleghenies and the Rocky Mountains, and the garden of Eden was on the east bank of the Mississippi River, between LaCrosse, Wisconsin, and Winona, Minnesota.

Jackson County, Missouri: Joseph Smith Jr. (1805-1844), founder of the Mormon Church, claimed the garden of Eden was situated near the city of Independence, Missouri.

WESLEY'S LAST LETTER

TO WILLIAM WILBERFORCE, ON HIS CAMPAIGN TO ABOLISH SLAVERY, 24 FEBRUARY 1791.

Dear Sir:

Unless the divine power has raised you up to be as "Athanasius against the world", I see not how you can go through your glorious enterprise in opposing that execrable villainy, which is the scandal of England, and of human nature. Unless God has raised you up for this very thing, you will be worn out by the opposition of men and devils. But if God be for you, who can be against you? Are all of them stronger than God? O be not weary of well doing! Go on, in the name of God and the power of His might, till even American slavery (the vilest that ever saw the sun) shall vanish away before it.

Reading this morning a tract by a poor African, I was especially struck by the circumstance, that a man who has a black skin, being wronged or outraged by a white man, can have no redress; it being a LAW in all our colonies that the OATH of a black man against a white goes for nothing. What villainy is this! That He who has guided you from youth up may continue to strengthen you in this and all things is the prayer of, dear sir,

Your affectionate servant,
John Wesley

"AIN'T I A WOMAN?"

If the man may preach, because the Savior died for him, why not the woman? seeing he died for her also. Is he not a whole Savior, instead of a half one?

—Jarena Lee (1783–1849), first authorized female
preacher in the African Methodist Episcopal Church

The poor men seem to be all in confusion, and don't know what to do. Why children, if you have woman's rights, give it to her and you will feel better. You will have your own rights, and they won't be so much trouble.

I can't read, but I can hear. I have heard the Bible and have learned that Eve caused man to sin. Well if woman upset the world, do give her a chance to set it right side up again.

—from "Ain't I a Woman?," Sojourner Truth
(c. 1797–1883), speech given on May 29, 1851;
transcribed by Marius Robinson June 21, 1851

ANGELOLOGY

According to the Roman Catholic Church, there are nine orders of angels. They are, in descending order:

1. Seraphim, or Fiery Ones
2. Cherubim
3. Thrones, or Many-Eyed Ones
4. Dominions, or Lordships
5. Virtues, or Brilliant/Shining Ones
6. Powers, or Warrior Angels
7. Principalities, Princedoms, or Rules
8. Archangels
9. Angels, or Guardian Angels

THE TEN OLDEST MEN IN THE BIBLE

Methuselah: 969 years (Gen. 5:21-27)
Jared: 962 years (Gen. 5:18-21)
Noah: 950 years (Gen. 9:29)
Adam: 930 years (Gen. 5:5)
Seth: 912 years (Gen. 5:8)
Cainan/Kenan: 910 years (Gen. 5:9-14)
Enos: 905 years (Gen. 5:6-11)
Mahaleel/Mahalel: 895 years (Gen. 5:12-17)
Lamech: 777 years (Gen. 5:31)
Enoch: 365 years—after which "he was not" (Gen. 5:18-24)

LOST AND FOUND

I missed him when the sun began to bend;
I found him not when I had lost his rim;
With many tears I went in search of him,
Climbing high mountains which did still ascend,
And gave me echoes when I called my friend;
Through cities vast and charnel-houses grim,

And high cathedrals where the light was dim,
Through books and arts and works without an end,
But found him not—the friend whom I had lost.
And yet I found him—as I found the lark,
A sound in fields I heard but could not mark;
I found him nearest when I missed him most;
I found him in my heart, a life in frost,
A light I knew not till my soul was dark.

—*George Macdonald (1824–1905)*

GOD'S PECULIAR PEOPLE

Wherever we find the Word of God surely preached and heard, and the sacraments administered according to the institution of Christ, there, it is not to be doubted, is a church of God.

—*John Calvin (1509–1564), Genevan reformer*

For one sect then to say, Ours is the true Church, and another say, Nay, but ours is the true Church, is as mad as to dispute whether your hall, or kitchen, or parlor, or coal-house is your house . . . when a child can tell them that the best is but a part, and the house contained them all.

—*Richard Baxter (1615–1691), English Puritan*

Churchgoers are like coals in a fire. When they cling together, they keep the flame aglow; when they separate, they die out.

—*Billy Graham (1918–2018), American evangelist*

Someone has said, "If we could get religion like a Baptist, experience it like a Methodist, be positive about it like a Disciple, be proud of it like an Episcopalian, pay for it like a Presbyterian, propagate it like an Adventist, and enjoy it like an Afro-American—that would be some religion!"

—*Harry Emerson Fosdick (1878–1969),*
American pastor

Going to church doesn't make you a Christian any more than going to the garage makes you a car.

> —*attributed to Moishe Rosen (1932–2010) and Laurence J. Peter (1919–1990), among others; frequently quoted by Billy Graham*

As I look around on Sunday morning at the people populating the pews, I see the risk that God has assumed. For whatever reason, God now reveals himself in the world not through a pillar of smoke and fire, not even through the physical body of his Son in Galilee, but through the mongrel collection that comprises my local church and every other such gathering in God's name.

> —*Philip Yancey (1949–), American author*

THE SHAKESPEARE PSALM

In the King James Version, the 46th word of Psalm 46 is "shake," and the 46th word from the end is "spear." When the King James Bible was being revised, in 1610, William Shakespeare was 46 years old.

Psalm 46

¹God is our refuge and strength, a very present help in trouble. ²Therefore will not we fear, though the earth be removed, and though the mountains be carried into the midst of the sea; ³Though the waters thereof roar and be troubled, though the mountains *shake* with the swelling thereof. ⁴There is a river, the streams whereof shall make glad the city of God, the holy place of the tabernacles of the most High. ⁵God is in the midst of her; she shall not be moved: God shall help her, and that right early. ⁶The heathen raged, the kingdoms were moved: he uttered his voice, the earth melted. ⁷The LORD of hosts is with us; the God of Jacob is our refuge. ⁸Come, behold the works of the LORD, what desolations he hath made in the earth. ⁹He maketh wars to cease unto the end of the earth; he breaketh the bow, and cutteth the *spear* in sunder;

he burneth the chariot in the fire. ¹⁰Be still, and know that I am God: I will be exalted among the heathen, I will be exalted in the earth. ¹¹The LORD of hosts is with us; the God of Jacob is our refuge.

UNSINGABLE HYMNS

By reason of my groaning voice
My bones cleave to my skin,
As pelican in wilderness
Such case now am I in.

—paraphrase of Psalm 102, Thomas Sternhold (1500–1549) and John Hopkins (d. 1570), English hymn publishers

Ye monsters of the bubbling deep
Your Maker's praises spout;
Up from the sands ye codlings peep,
And wag your tails about.

—risible paraphrase of Psalm 148, Cotton Mather (1663–1728), Puritan minister

Be Thou, O Lord, the rider
And we the little ass,
That to God's holy city
Together we may pass.

—omitted verse of "All Glory, Laud and Honor," John Mason Neale (1818–1866), Anglican hymn writer

O may thy powerful word
Inspire the feeble worm
To rush into thy kingdom, Lord,
And take it as by storm.

—from the Wesleyan Hymn Book

What though the spicy breezes
    Blow soft o'er Ceylon's isle,

Though every prospect pleases,
    And only man is vile!
In vain with lavish kindness
    The gifts of God are strewn;
The heathen in his blindness
    Bows down to wood and stone.

—from missionary hymn "From Greenland's Icy Mountains," Reginald Heber (1783-1826), English hymn writer

I wish to have no wishes left,
But to leave all to Thee;
And yet I wish that Thou should'st will
That which I wish should be.

—from a hymn by Frederick William Faber (1814-1863), English hymn writer

BIBLE ANIMALS

In its original languages, the Bible uses twelve different words for "sheep" and ten for "cattle."

Like the children of Israel, working animals such as donkeys and oxen were to rest on the Sabbath (Exod. 23:12).

The domestic cat is never mentioned in the Bible.

The King James Version mentions unicorns twelve times. The Hebrew original probably means "auroch" rather than the creature of legend.

"Leviathan" (Hebrew *livyatan*, Job 41:1 in English translations; Hebrew 40:25) probably refers to the crocodile.

"Behemoth" (Hebrew *behemot*, Job 40:15) probably means hippopotamus—or perhaps elephant.

Legend has it that the donkey has borne a dark cross on its back ever since Jesus rode one into Jerusalem on Palm Sunday, a week before he was crucified (Matt. 21:2).

SPOONERISMS

Spoonerism: an error in speech where consonants or vowels are swapped between two words in a phrase. Named after the albino and absent-minded Oxford academic Rev. William Archibald Spooner (1844-1930), who was renowned for this habit.

Kinquering congs their titles take.

The Lord is a shoving leopard.

The Lord will tease my ears.

Satan tells a lack of pies.

Take unto you the shield of faith, wherewith you are able to quench all the direy farts of the devil!

The tearful chidings of the gospel.

You are occupewing my pie.

NOAH'S ARK JOKES

Why were there no card games on the ark?
Because Noah sat on the deck.

How did Noah illuminate the ark?
With flood lights.

What do we call the study of Noah's ark?
Arkeology.

Was Noah the first one out of the ark?
No! He came forth out of the ark.

Which creature took most luggage into the ark?
The elephant—he took his trunk.

Why were there no worms in the ark?
Because worms come in apples not in pairs.

Where did Noah keep the bees?
In the ark-hives.

Why did Noah punish the chickens on the ark?
Because they were using fowl language.

Where is meat first mentioned in the Bible?
When Noah took Ham into the ark.

GREAT OPENING LINES OF SCRIPTURE

In the beginning God created the heaven and the earth.

—Genesis

Adam, Sheth, Enosh, Kenan, Mahalaleel, Jered, Henoch, Methuselah, Lamech, Noah, Shem, Ham, and Japheth.

—1 Chronicles

Now it came to pass in the thirtieth year, in the fourth month, in the fifth day of the month, as I was among the captives by the river of Chebar, that the heavens were opened, and I saw visions of God.

—Ezekiel

In the beginning was the Word, and the Word was with God, and the Word was God.

—John

God, who at sundry times and in divers manners spake in time past unto the fathers by the prophets, hath in these last days spoken unto us by his Son.

—Hebrews

That which was from the beginning, which we have heard, which we have seen with our eyes, which we have looked upon, and our hands have handled, of the Word of life.

—1 John

The Revelation of Jesus Christ, which God gave unto him, to shew unto his servants things which must shortly come to pass; and he sent and signified it by his angel unto his servant John.

—Revelation

MERCY

The quality of mercy is not strained,
It droppeth as the gentle rain from heaven
Upon the place beneath. It is twice blest,
It blesseth him that gives, and him that takes,
'Tis mightiest in the mightiest. It becomes
The thronèd monarch better than his crown.
His sceptre shows the force of temporal power,
The attribute to awe and majesty,
Wherein doth sit the dread and fear of kings;
But mercy is above this sceptred sway,
It is enthronèd in the hearts of kings,
It is an attribute to God himself,

And earthly power doth then show likest God's
When mercy seasons justice.

> *—from* The Merchant of Venice, *Act 4, Scene 1,*
> *William Shakespeare*

BIBLE NAMES BEST NOT GIVEN TO YOUR CHILDREN

Cain	Judas
Herod	Pilate
Mephibosheth	Dodo (2 Sam. 23:24)
Jezebel	

PEACE IN OUR TIME

Most merciful God, the Granter of all peace and quietness, the Giver of all good gifts, the Defender of all nations, who hast willed all men to be accounted as our neighbours, and commanded us to love them as ourself, and not to hate our enemies, but rather to wish them, yea and also to do them good if we can. . . . Give to all us desire of peace, unity, and quietness, and a speedy wearisomeness of all war, hostility, and enmity to all them that be our enemies; that we and they may, in one heart and charitable agreement, praise thy most holy name, and reform our lives to thy godly commandments.

> *—Thomas Cranmer (1489–1556), English reformer,*
> *in 1548, when England was at war with Scotland*

HOW THE BIBLE WAS DIVIDED UP

Archbishop of Canterbury Stephen Langton (c. 1150–1228) is believed first to have divided the Bible into chapters.

Mordecai Nathan of Avignon divided the Hebrew Old Testament into verses around 1448. Previously, verse divisions had been marked by dots.

Robert Estienne (1503–1559), a refugee in Geneva, in 1551 first printed a New Testament (in Latin and Greek) with the verse divisions in use today.

The first English New Testament to use these verse divisions was the Geneva Version (1560).

Legend has it the verses were initially marked up in a moving carriage, accounting for the uneven verse lengths and occasional midsentence divisions.

"THE LAMB"

    Little Lamb, who made thee?
    Dost thou know who made thee?
Gave thee life and bid thee feed
By the stream and o'er the mead;
Gave thee clothing of delight,
Softest clothing, wooly bright;
Gave thee such a tender voice,
Making all the vales rejoice?
    Little Lamb, who made thee?
    Dost thou know who made thee?

    Little Lamb, I'll tell thee,
    Little Lamb, I'll tell thee!
He is calléd by thy name,
For he calls himself a Lamb;
He is meek and he is mild,
He became a little child:
I a child and thou a lamb,
We are calléd by his name.
    Little Lamb, God bless thee.
    Little Lamb, God bless thee.

—*William Blake (1757–1827),*
English poet and painter

ON SCRIPTURE

The holy scriptures are our letters from home.

—*Augustine of Hippo (354–430),*
North African theologian

I have found in the Bible words for my inmost thoughts, songs for my joy, utterances for my hidden griefs, and pleadings for my shame and my feebleness.

—*Samuel Taylor Coleridge (1772–1834),*
English Romantic poet

The first and almost the only book deserving of universal attention is the Bible. I speak as a man of the world . . . and I say to you, "Search the Scriptures."

John Quincy Adams (1767–1848), US president

Christian, noun: one who believes that the New Testament is a divinely inspired book admirably suited to the spiritual needs of his neighbor.

—*from* The Devil's Dictionary,
Ambrose Bierce (1842?–1914), American writer

This Bible is for the Government of the People, by the People, and for the People.

—*John Wycliffe (c. 1320–1384), English theologian,*
possibly referenced in Abraham Lincoln's
Gettysburg Address (1863)

The Bible, the whole Bible, and nothing but the Bible is the religion of Christ's church.

—*Charles Haddon Spurgeon (1834–1892),*
English Baptist preacher

Most people are bothered by those passages in Scripture which they cannot understand; but as for me, I always noticed that the passages in Scripture which trouble me most are those that I do understand.

—*Mark Twain (1835–1910), American author*

CARELESS CONFIRMATION

When I was a schoolboy about fifteen years of age, the Bishop coming into the country, many went to be confirmed. We that were boys ran out to see the Bishop among the rest, not knowing anything of the meaning of the business. When we came thither, we met about thirty or forty in all, of our own stature and temper, that had come for us to be "bishopped," as then it was called. The Bishop examined us not at all in one article of the Faith; but in a churchyard in haste we were set in rank, and he passed hastily over us, laying his hands on our head, and saying a few words, which neither I nor any that I spoke with, understood; so hastily were they uttered and a very short prayer recited, and there was an end. But whether we were Christians or infidels, or knew as much as that there was a God, the Bishop little knew or inquired. . . . This was the old careless practice of this excellent duty of Confirmation.

—*Richard Baxter (1615–1691), English Puritan*

A CITY ON A HILL

We must entertain each other in brotherly affection. . . . We must uphold a familiar commerce together in all meekness, gentleness, patience and liberality. We must delight in each other; make others' conditions our own; rejoice together, mourn together, labor and suffer together, always having before our eyes our commission and community in the work, as members of the same body. So shall we keep the unity of the spirit in the bond of peace. The Lord will be our God, and delight to dwell among us, as His own people, and will command a blessing upon us in all our ways, so that we shall see much more of His wisdom, power, goodness and truth, than formerly we have been acquainted with. We shall find that the God of Israel is among us, when ten of us shall be able to resist a thousand of our enemies; when He shall make us a praise and glory that men shall say of succeeding plantations, "may the Lord make it like that of New England." *For we must consider that we shall be as a city upon a hill. . . .*

> *Therefore let us choose life,*
> *that we and our seed may live,*
> *by obeying His voice and cleaving to Him,*
> *for He is our life and our prosperity.*

—John Winthrop (1588-1649), in the 1630 sermon "A Model of Christian Clarity"

THE TEN PLAGUES OF EGYPT

1. Water in the river turns to blood (Exod. 7:20)
2. Frogs cover the land (Exod. 8:6)
3. Lice—or gnats—infest humans and animals (Exod. 8:17)
4. Swarms of flies ruin the land (Exod. 8:24)
5. Murrain destroys cattle and other livestock (Exod. 9:6)
6. Boils and sores erupt on animals and humans (Exod. 9:10)
7. Tumultuous, fiery hailstorm (Exod. 9:23)
8. Locusts devour every green thing (Exod. 10:15)
9. Darkness covers the land for three days (Exod. 10:22)
10. Firstborn of Egyptian people and cattle die (Exod. 11:5)

THE BEATITUDES

Taught to Jesus's followers in the Sermon on the Mount.

Blessed are the poor in spirit: for theirs is the kingdom of heaven.
Blessed are they that mourn: for they shall be comforted.
Blessed are the meek: for they shall inherit the earth.

Blessed are they which do hunger and thirst after righteousness: for they shall be filled.

Blessed are the merciful: for they shall obtain mercy.

Blessed are the pure of heart: for they shall see God.

Blessed are the peacemakers: for they shall be called the children of God.

Blessed are they which are persecuted for righteousness' sake: for theirs is the kingdom of heaven.

Blessed are ye, when men shall revile you, and persecute you, and shall say all manner of evil against you falsely, for my sake.

Rejoice, and be exceeding glad: for great is your reward in heaven: for so persecuted they the prophets which were before you. (Matt. 5:3–12)

HOW TO ELECT A POPE

The pope, or "Holy Father," is the bishop of Rome, elected by the clergy of his diocese.

Because he oversees the Roman Catholic Church worldwide, priests of the Diocese of Rome—the College of Cardinals—are drawn from across the Catholic Church, most being bishops or archbishops.

Pope John Paul II revised the rules for electing a pope. Cardinals must be younger than eighty years old to vote, and their number is limited to 120. When a pope dies, this "conclave" of cardinals spends two or three weeks in mourning before gathering in the Vatican's Sistine Chapel.

The electors write their choice on a secret ballot and are isolated from the outside world and sworn to secrecy about their discussions. The winning candidate must receive at least two-thirds of the votes. However, after thirty inconclusive ballots, a simple majority is sufficient. After each vote, the paper ballots are burned, the smoke signaling to the world outside. If a pope has been elected, a substance that creates white smoke is used.

The new pope next chooses the name he will take, after which the dean of the College of Cardinals introduces him from the main balcony of the Vatican, declaring "*Habemus Papam*" – "We have a pope!"

SERENITY

Serenity Prayer

God, grant me the serenity to accept the things I cannot change;
the courage to change the things I can;
and the wisdom to know the difference.

This is probably based on an original prayer by American theologian Reinhold Niebuhr (1892–1971):

Father, give us courage to change what must be altered,
serenity to accept what cannot be helped,
and the insight to know the one from the other.

Antiserenity Prayer

God, grant me the anxiety to try to control things I cannot control,
the fear to avoid the things I can,
and the neurosis to deny the difference.

Senility Prayer

God, grant me the senility to forget the people I never liked anyway,
the good fortune to run into the ones I do,
and the eyesight to tell the difference.

THE DAILY OFFICE

The hours of prayer in a monastery, customarily known as the Daily Office:

Matins	Middle of the night, or before retiring
Lauds	After matins, or early morning
Prime (first)	Around 6:00 a.m.
Terce (third)	Around 9:00 a.m.
Sext (sixth)	Around noon
None (ninth)	Around 3:00 p.m.
Vespers	Before dark
Compline	Before retiring

ANGELS

The book of 1 Enoch, not included in the Bibles of most Christian churches, was supposedly written by Enoch, the father of Methuselah (see Gen. 5:21). It includes the following angels:

Archangel Michael (Dan. 12:1; Jude 9; Rev. 12:7; Enoch)
Gabriel (Dan. 8:16; Luke 1:19, 26; Enoch)
Raphael (Tob. 3:17; Enoch): over the spirits of men
Uriel (Enoch): over the world and "Tartarus"
Raguel (Enoch): takes vengeance on the world of luminaries
Saraquel (Enoch): set over the spirits
Remiel (Enoch): set over those "who rise"

THE SHEPHERD PSALM

Probably the best known and most loved of the psalms, this has been set to music many times as a hymn and an anthem, and is frequently spoken or sung at funerals.

¹The Lord is my shepherd; I shall not want. ²He maketh me to lie down in green pastures: he leadeth me beside the still waters. ³He restoreth my soul: he leadeth me in the paths of righteousness for his name's sake. ⁴Yea, though I walk through the valley of the shadow of death, I will fear no evil: for thou art with me; thy rod and thy staff they comfort me. ⁵Thou preparest a table before me in the presence of mine enemies: thou anointest my head with oil; my cup runneth over. ⁶Surely goodness and mercy shall follow me all the days of my life: and I will dwell in the house of the Lord for ever. (Ps. 23)

Middle English version in Wycliffe's Bible, 1392–1395

The Lord gouerneth me, and no thing schal faile to me;
²in the place of pasture there he hath set me. He nurschide me on the watir of refreischyng;
³he conuertide my soule. He ledde me forth on the pathis of riytfulnesse; for his name.
⁴For whi thouy Y schal go in the myddis of schadewe of deeth; Y schal not drede yuels, for thou art with me. Thi yerde and thi staf; tho han coumfortid me.
⁵Thou hast maad redi a boord in my siyt; ayens hem that troblen me. Thou hast maad fat myn heed with oyle; and my cuppe, fillinge greetli, is ful cleer.
⁶And thi merci schal sue me; in alle the daies of my lijf. And that Y dwelle in the hows of the Lord; in to the lengthe of daies.

SOME BIBLE HOWLERS

Noah's wife was called Joan of Ark.

Lot's wife was a pillar of salt by day—but a ball of fire by night.

Samson slew the Philistines with the axe of the apostles.

The Egyptians all drowned in the dessert.

Moses went up Mount Cyanide to get the Ten Amendments.

The fifth commandment is "Humor thy father and mother."

The seventh commandment is thou shalt not admit adultery.

David was a king skilled at playing the liar.

King Solomon had 300 wives and 700 porcupines.

When Mary heard she was the mother of Jesus she sang the Magna Carta.

Jesus spoke Aromatic.

The men who followed Jesus were called the Twelve Decibels.

A parable is a heavenly story with no earthly meaning.

The epistles were the wives of the apostles.

At the Last Supper the disciples ate unleaded bread.

ATHEIST'S HYMN

Lord, Lord, I don't believe in you,
I only believe in me.
Lord, your miracles I've never seen,
Only your earth and sea.
Lord, I know not your heaven or hell,
Only those which burn in me.
Lord, I wish to stand and shout from the hills,
Not mutter on bended knee.

Lord, Lord, I have only one prayer,
Which I cry irreverently:
Let me make music all my life long
Which reminds men of thee.

—Anonymous

BANNED!

Some notables excommunicated by the church:

> *Pope Leo IX* and *Michael I Cerularius*, patriarch of Constantinople, excommunicated each other in 1054—leading to the major breach between the Eastern and Western churches.
>
> *King Henry VIII*—excommunicated by Pope Clement VII in 1533 for annulling his marriage to Catherine of Aragon and marrying Anne Boleyn.
>
> *Martin Luther*, German reformer—excommunicated by Pope Leo X in 1521.
>
> *Elizabeth I of England*—excommunicated by Pope Pius V in 1570 for claiming to be head of the church in England.
>
> *Leo Tolstoy*, author of *War and Peace*—excommunicated by the Russian Holy Synod in 1901 for his unorthodox beliefs.
>
> *Nikos Kazantzakis*—excommunicated by the Greek Orthodox Church in 1954 for his novel *The Last Temptation of Christ*.
>
> *Juan Perón*, Argentine dictator—excommunicated in 1955 for legalizing divorce and prostitution.

LUTHER AT THE DIET OF WORMS

The reformer rejects papal authority:

> Your Imperial Majesty and Your Lordships demand a simple answer. Here it is, plain and unvarnished. Unless I am convicted [convinced] of error by the testimony of Scripture or (since I put no trust in the unsupported authority of Pope or councils, since it is plain that they have often erred and often

contradicted themselves) by manifest reasoning, I stand convicted by the Scriptures to which I have appealed, and my conscience is taken captive by God's word, I cannot and will not recant anything, for to act against our conscience is neither safe for us, nor open to us.

On this I take my stand. I can do no other. God help me. Amen.

—from Documents of the Christian Church (1903),
H. C. Bettenson

POPULAR WEDDING MUSIC

Prelude

"Canon in D," Johann Pachelbel
"Holsworthy Church Bells," Samuel Sebastian Wesley
"Nimrod," from *Enigma Variations*, Edward Elgar
"Greensleeves," trad. English

Processional

"Wedding March," from *Lohengrin*, Richard Wagner
"Arrival of the Queen of Sheba," from *Solomon*, George Frideric Handel
"Wedding March," Felix Mendelssohn
"Trumpet Voluntary," John Stanley
"I Was Glad," Hubert Parry
"Hornpipe," from *Water Music*, George Frideric Handel

Signing the Register

"Sheep May Safely Graze," J. S. Bach
"Jesu, Joy of Man's Desiring," J. S. Bach
"*Exultate Jubilate*," W. A. Mozart
"The Lord Bless You and Keep You," John Rutter
"*Ave Verum Corpus*," W. A. Mozart

Recessional

"Grand March," from *Le Prophète*, Giacomo Meyerbeer
"March," from *Scipio*, George Frideric Handel
"Hallelujah Chorus," from *Messiah*, George Frideric Handel

HAND AND EYE

The Christian shoemaker does his duty not by putting little crosses on the shoes but by making good shoes, because God is interested in good craftsmanship.

—*Martin Luther (1483–1546), German reformer*

God be praised,
Antonio Stradivari has an eye
That winces at false work and loves the true. . . .
". . . for my fame—when any master holds
'Twixt chin and hand a violin of mine,
He will be glad that Stradivari lived,
Made violins, and made them of the best. . . .
I say not God himself can make man's best
Without best men to help him. . . .
 'Tis God gives skill,
But not without men's hands: he could not make
Antonio Stradivari's violins
Without Antonio."

—*edited from "Stradivarius," George Eliot
(Mary Ann Evans, 1819–1880), English author*

CORNY CHURCH ADS

Seven prayerless days make one weak

Danger! Live church!

Sing a hymn for Him

Fight truth decay!
Brush up your Bible every day.

Happy Easter to our Christian friends
Happy Passover to our Jewish friends
To our atheist friends . . . Good Luck!

Now open Sundays!

We are the soul agents in this area

God is perfect . . .
Only man makes misteaks!

Can't sleep?
Don't count sheep—talk to the Shepherd!

As you pass this little church,
be sure to plan a visit
So when at last you're carried in
God won't ask "Who is it?"

JESUS'S FINAL WEEK

Sunday	Palm Sunday
	Jesus's triumphal entry into Jerusalem (Matt. 21:1-11)
Monday	Jesus cleanses the temple (Mark 11:15-19)
Tuesday	Jesus teaches on the Mount of Olives (Matt. 24:3-25:46)
Thursday	Maundy Thursday
	Jesus celebrates the Last Supper with his disciples (Matt. 26:17-30)
	Jesus is betrayed, arrested (Mark 14:43-72), and tried (John 18:28–19:16)

Friday	Good Friday
	Jesus is crucified and buried (Matt. 27:32–61)
Saturday	Low Saturday
Sunday	Easter Day
	Jesus rises from the dead and appears to his disciples (Luke 24:1–43)

AN EASY LIFE?

What was Christ's life? Not one of deep speculations, quiet thoughts, and bright visions . . . but a life of fighting against evil; earnest, awful prayers and struggles within, continued labor of body and mind without; insult and danger, and confusion, and violent exertion, and bitter sorrow. This was Christ's life.

—from Twenty-Five Village Sermons, *sermon 15: "The Transfiguration," by Charles Kingsley (1819–1875), English clergyman and novelist*

The love of God did not protect His own Son. . . . He will not necessarily protect us—not from anything it takes to make us like His Son.

—Elisabeth Elliot (1926–2015), missionary

If you want a religion to make you feel really comfortable, I certainly don't recommend Christianity.

—C. S. Lewis (1898–1963), English writer

Some people think reconciliation is a soft option, that it means papering over the cracks. But the biblical meaning means looking facts in the face and it can be very costly: it cost God the death of his own Son.

—Desmond Tutu (1931–), South African theologian

SEASONS

To every thing there is a season, and a time to every purpose under the heaven:
A time to be born, and a time to die; a time to plant, and a time to pluck up that which is planted;
A time to kill, and a time to heal; a time to break down, and a time to build up;
A time to weep, and a time to laugh; a time to mourn, and a time to dance;
A time to cast away stones, and a time to gather stones together; a time to embrace, and a time to refrain from embracing;
A time to get, and a time to lose; a time to keep, and a time to cast away;
A time to rend, and a time to sew; a time to keep silence, and a time to speak;
A time to love, and a time to hate; a time of war, and a time of peace.

—*Ecclesiastes 3:1–8*

"I AM"

I am—yet what I am none cares or knows;
My friends forsake me like a memory lost:
I am the self-consumer of my woes—
They rise and vanish in oblivious host,
Like shadows in love's frenzied throes
And yet I am, and live—like vapours tossed

Into the nothingness of scorn and noise,
Into the living sea of waking dreams,
While there is neither sense of life nor joys,
But the vast shipwreck of my life's esteems;
Even the dearest that I loved the best
Are strange—nay, rather, stranger than the rest.

I long for scenes where man has never trod
A place where woman never smiled or wept.
There to abide with my Creator, God,
And sleep as I in childhood sweetly slept,
Untroubling and untroubled where I lie
The grass below—above the vaulted sky.

—*John Clare (1793-1864)*

TEN SONGS REFERENCING "AMAZING GRACE"

"'Amazing Grace' Used to Be Her Favorite Song," by Russell Smith, 1974

"Foot of Pride," by Bob Dylan, 1983: "Sing 'Amazing Grace' all the way to the Swiss banks"

"Pretty Amazing Grace," by Neil Diamond, 2008

"She Sings Amazing Grace," by Jerry Lee Lewis, 1983

"Shadrach," by the Beastie Boys, 1988: "I once was lost, but now I'm found"

"The President Sang Amazing Grace," by Joan Baez, 2018

"A Long Walk," by Jill Scott, 2000: "I was blind, now I can see"

"The Crawl," by Placebo, 1998: "Amazing grace in here I'd pay to have you near"

"American Dream," by Afroman, 2000: quotes entire first stanza

"The Bravest," by Tom Paxton, 2001: tribute to 9/11 firefighters: "The pipers play 'Amazing Grace,' as the coffins come in view"

BIBLICAL BOTTLES

Outsize wine bottles known by Bible names:

Jeroboam: equivalent to 4 regular bottles (3 liters). First king of the Northern Kingdom of Israel (1 Kings 11:31).

Rehoboam: equivalent to 6 bottles. First king of the Southern Kingdom of Israel (1 Kings 11:43).

Methuselah: equivalent to 8 bottles. Oldest man in the Old Testament (Gen. 5:27).

Shalmaneser/Salmanazar: equivalent to 12 bottles. King of Assyria (2 Kings 17:3).

Balthazar: equivalent to 16 bottles. Traditional name for one of the Magi (Matt. 2:1).

Nebuchadnezzar: equivalent to 20 bottles. King of Babylon (2 Kings 24:1).

Melchior: equivalent to 24 bottles. Legendary name for another of the Magi.

Solomon: equivalent to 28 bottles. King of Israel (1 Kings 2:12).

Melchizedek: equivalent to 40 bottles. King of Salem (Gen. 14:18).

JOHN WESLEY'S HEART WARMED

I think it was about five this morning that I opened my Testament on those words: "There are given unto us exceeding great and precious promises, even that you should be partakers of the divine nature." Just as I went out, I opened it again on those words, "You are not far from the kingdom of God." In the afternoon I was asked to go to St. Paul's. The anthem was "Out of the deep have I called unto you, O Lord: Lord, hear my voice."

In the evening I went very unwillingly to a society in Aldersgate Street, where one was reading Luther's preface to the Epistle to the Romans. About a quarter before nine, while he was describing the change which God works in the heart through faith in Christ, I felt my heart strangely warmed. I felt I did trust in Christ, Christ alone, for salvation: and an assurance was given me that he had taken away my sins, even mine, and saved me from the law of sin and death.

—from Journal, *John Wesley,*
Wednesday, May 24, 1738

COMPLAINT

Still I complain; I am complaining still.
Oh! woe is me! Was ever Heart like mine?
A Sty of Filth, a Trough of Washing-Swill,
A Dunghill Pit, a Puddle of mere Slime.
A Nest of Vipers, Hive of Hornets' Stings.
A Bag of Poyson, Civit-Box of Sins.

—from Preparatory Meditations, *Edward Taylor (c. 1642–1729), American poet*

A GATHERING OF BRITISH SAINTS

- *St. Alban* (third century), first British Christian martyr. Alban is said to have been beheaded at Roman Verulamium, later renamed St. Albans.
- *St. David* (c. 500–589), patron saint of Wales. Buried in St. David's Cathedral, Pembrokeshire.
- *St. Cuthbert* (c. 634–687), bishop of Lindisfarne. Durham Cathedral was built over his last resting place.
- *St. Bede* (c. 672–735), Northumbrian monk known as "the Venerable Bede." The first English historian, author of *The Ecclesiastical History of the English People*.
- *St. Columba* (521–597), Irish-born founder of Iona monastery, from which much of Scotland was converted.
- *St. Thomas More* (1478–1535), Henry VIII's lord chancellor, executed for opposing the king's divorce.
- *St. Swithun* (c. 800–863), bishop of Winchester. It's said that if it rains on his feast day, it will rain the next forty days.
- *St. Edmund* (841–869), king of East Anglia, martyred by being shot with arrows and beheaded. His tomb, at Bury St. Edmunds, became a popular shrine.
- *St. Thomas Becket* (c. 1118–1170), archbishop of Canterbury, murdered in his cathedral at the supposed wish of Henry II.
- *St. Charles the Martyr* (1600–1649), Stuart monarch, executed in 1649.

TIME'S PACES

When, as a child, I laughed and wept,
 Time crept.
When, as a youth, I waxed more bold,
 Time walked.
When I became a full-grown man,
 Time strolled.
When older still I daily grew,
 Time FLEW.
Soon I shall find, in passing on,
 Time *gone*.
Oh Christ! wilt Thou have saved me then?
 Amen.

> —*from* Hymns and Other Stray Verses, *Henry Twells
> (1823–1900), Anglican clergyman and poet,
> on a clock in Chester Cathedral, England*

BIBLIOMANCY

Bibliomancy is the practice of foretelling the future by choosing randomly a passage in a book. The book chosen is often the Bible, and the hope is of receiving a message from God.

One method is to close one's eyes and open the Bible at random—or balance it on its spine and let it fall open. With the eyes still closed, place a finger on the open page to select the words to read.

And take care: remember the apocryphal story of the person who opened his Bible and placed his finger on Matthew 27:5: "Judas went away and hanged himself." "That can't be right," thought he, so he tried again. This time he opened at Luke 10:37: "Jesus told him, 'Go and do likewise.'"

"DAY BY DAY"

Day by day, dear Lord,
of thee three things I pray:

to see thee more clearly,
love thee more dearly,
follow thee more nearly,
day by day.

> —*attributed to Richard, bishop of Chichester (1197-1253), popularized in a folk-rock setting in Godspell (1971), the musical by Stephen Schwartz and John-Michael Tebelak*

SOME BIBLE FIRSTS

First man: Adam
First woman: Eve
First child: Cain
First death: Abel
First person not to die: Enoch
First clothes: aprons of fig leaves
First boat: the ark
First drunk: Noah
First twins: Esau and Jacob
First king: Melchizedek of Salem
First king of Israel: Abimelech
First disciples of Jesus: Peter and Andrew
First of Jesus's miracles: turning water to wine at Cana
First Christian martyr: Stephen

THE GATE OF THE YEAR

King George VI's first Christmas Day radio broadcast of World War II, December 25, 1939, included these resonant words by the British poet Minnie Louise Haskins (1875-1957) from her poem "God Knows":

"I said to the man who stood at the Gate of the Year, 'Give me a light that I may tread safely into the unknown.' And he replied, 'Go out into the darkness, and put your hand into the Hand of God. That shall be to you better than light, and safer than a known way.'"

THE RIGHT HYMN FOR THE JOB

Hymns for particular callings:

> *The Dentist's Hymn*: "Crown Him with Many Crowns"
> *The Meteorologist's Hymn*: "There Shall Be Showers of Blessing"
> *The Builder's Hymn*: "The Church's One Foundation"
> *The Tailor's Hymn*: "Holy, Holy, Holy"
> *The Golfer's Hymn*: "There Is a Green Hill Far Away"
> *The Politician's Hymn*: "Standing on the Promises"
> *The Optician's Hymn*: "Open Mine Eyes That I May See"
> *The Astronaut's Hymn*: "Nearer, My God, to Thee"
> *The Fisherman's Hymn*: "Shall We Gather at the River?"
> *The Historian's Hymn*: "Tell Me the Old, Old Story"

"WHAT IS DYING?"

Also known as "Gone from My Sight" and the "Parable of Immortality."

> I am standing upon the seashore.
> A ship at my side spreads her white sails to the morning breeze, and starts for the blue ocean.
> She is an object of beauty and strength,
> and I stand and watch her until she hangs like a speck of white cloud
> just where the sea and sky come down to mingle with each other.
> Then someone at my side says: "There! She's gone!"
> Gone where? Gone from my sight—that is all.
> She is just as large in mast and hull and spar as she was when she left my side,

and just as able to bear her load of living freight
to the place of her destination.
Her diminished size is in me, and not in her.

And just at the moment
when someone at my side says: "There! She's gone!"
there are other eyes that are watching for her coming;
and other voices ready to take up the glad shout:
"There she comes!"

> —*probably by Rev. Luther F. Beecher (1813–1903), cousin of Harriet Beecher Stowe (author of* Uncle Tom's Cabin), *though often attributed to Henry Van Dyke and Bishop Charles Brent*

THE APOCRYPHA

Jerome revised the Latin Bible to produce the version we know as the Vulgate. He removed from the Old Testament any books not in the Hebrew Bible, calling them "apocrypha," that is, of dubious authenticity.

The Roman Catholic Church accepted most of these books as belonging to a secondary "canon," that is, "deuterocanonical." These fourteen books are usually included in Roman Catholic Bibles, interspersed with the other Old Testament books. They are not normally found in Bibles used by Protestants.

1 Esdras
2 Esdras
Tobit
Judith
Additions to the Book of Esther
The Wisdom of Solomon
Ecclesiasticus (Sirach)
Baruch (with the Epistle of Jeremiah)
Prayer of Azariah (The Song of the Three Holy Children)
The History of Susanna

Bel and the Dragon
The Prayer of Manasseh
1 Maccabees
2 Maccabees

BIBLE GIANTS

Og, king of Bashan, one of "the remnant of the giants, that dwelt at Ashtaroth and at Edrei" (Josh. 12:4). He possessed an iron—or possibly stone—bedstead, nine cubits long and four cubits wide (roughly 13 feet by 6 feet, or 4 meters by 2 meters).

Goliath, the giant Philistine killed by David. His height is given in 1 Samuel 17:4 as six cubits and a span (about 10 feet, or almost 3 meters).

An Egyptian giant five cubits tall, mentioned in 1 Chronicles 11:23, owned a spear "like a weaver's beam."

Three Philistine giants are mentioned in 1 Chronicles 20, one of whom had six fingers on each hand, six toes on each foot (v. 6).

THE PRESBYTERIAN CAT

There was a Presbyterian cat
Went searching for her prey,
And found a moose within the hoose,
Upon the Sawbath day.

The people were all horrifiet,
And they were grieved sair,
And straightway led that wicked cat
Before the ministaire.

The ministaire was horrifiet
And unto her did say:
"Oh, naughty cat to catch a moose,
Upon the Sawbath day."

"The Sawbath's been, fra days of yore,
An institution."
So they straightway led the wicked cat
to execution.

—Anonymous, *a traditional Scots song,
mocking strict Sabbatarians*

LIFE ON EARTH

The present life of man on earth, O king, when compared with the entire length of time that is unknown to us, seems to me like the swift flight of a sparrow through the hall where you sit at dinner by a good fire with your chiefs and ministers in wintertime, while rain and snowstorms rage outside. It flies in one door and immediately out through another; while inside, it is safe from the wintry storm; but after a brief period of calm, it vanishes into the dark winter from which it appeared. Man's life on earth seems to be rather like this; we are utterly ignorant about what preceded it and what will follow. So if this new teaching contains something more certain, it seems right we should follow it.

—*paraphrase of Venerable Bede's presentation
of Christianity to King Edwin of Northumbria*

PEACE

Drop thy still dews of quietness.
Till all our strivings cease;

Take from our souls the strain and stress.
And let our ordered lives confess
The beauty of thy peace.

> *—from "The Brewing of Soma,"*
> *John Greenleaf Whittier (1807–1892), American poet*

TEN MOVIES ABOUT FAITH, DOUBT, AND SIN

The Nun's Story (1959), directed by Fred Zinnemann, starring Audrey Hepburn. Cloistered nuns and their struggle to obey their vows.

The Cardinal (1963), directed by Otto Preminger. A priest's crisis of faith on the eve of World War II, based on the life of Cardinal Spellman, archbishop of New York. Vatican liaison officer: Joseph Ratzinger, later Pope Benedict XVI

Agnes of God (1985), directed by Norman Jewison. A psychiatrist (Jane Fonda) investigates a nun whose infant is found strangled and who claims a virgin conception.

The Last Temptation of Christ (1988), directed by Martin Scorsese. Jesus (Willem Dafoe) abandons God's plan and lives with Mary Magdalene, but with Jerusalem burning, finds himself back on the cross.

Doubt (2008), directed by John Patrick Shanley, starring Meryl Streep and Philip Seymour Hoffman. A Catholic sister suspects a priest has a relationship with a black altar boy.

We Have a Pope (*Habemus Papam*, 2011), directed by Nanni Moretti. French comedy-drama about a cardinal elected pope against his wishes.

Spotlight (2015), directed by Tom McCarthy. The *Boston Globe*'s "Spotlight" team uncovers child sex abuse by Roman Catholic priests.

Silence (2016), directed by Martin Scorsese. Portuguese Jesuit missionaries in Edo-era Japan, where believers are martyred for their faith.

By the Grace of God (*Grâce à Dieu*, 2018), directed by François Ozon. Based on a true incident of three men's campaign to expose a priest's child abuse.

The Two Popes (2019), directed by Fernando Meirelles, starring Jonathan Price and Anthony Hopkins. Fictional conversations of Popes Francis and Benedict XVI before the latter abdicated.

SOME BIBLE MISPRINTS

A number of Bibles have been given nicknames based on a typographical error, odd wording, or mistranslation.

Bug Bible (Myles Coverdale's Bible, 1535)
Psalm 91:5 reads, "Thou shalt not nede to be afrayed for eny bugges by night." The King James Version translates as "terror."

Treacle Bible (Great Bible, 1549)
Jeremiah 8:22 reads, "Is there no tryacle [treacle] in Gilead?"—rather than "balm." In its period, this was not, strictly speaking, an error: "treacle" was another word for ointment, balm. (The 1632 KJV reads, "Is there no blame in Gilead?")

Placemaker's Bible (Geneva Bible, 1562)
Matthew 5:9 reads, "Blessed are the placemakers" instead of "peacemakers."

Breeches Bible (Geneva Bible, 1579)
Genesis 3:7 reads that Adam and Eve "sewed fig tree leaves together, and made themselves breeches." The KJV has "aprons."

Printers' Bible (KJV, 1612)
Psalm 119:161, "princes have persecuted me without cause," ap-

pears as "printers have persecuted me without cause." Perhaps a Freudian slip or deliberate error?

Wicked, Sinners', or Adulterous Bible (KJV, 1631)
The sixth commandment reads: "Thou shalt commit adultery" (Exod. 20:14). Most copies were recalled and destroyed: eleven are known to survive. The publishers, Robert Barker and Martin Lucas, were fined £300 for the error—a huge sum for the time. It has been suggested that the error was deliberate sabotage, to deprive the publishers of their license to print Bibles.

Vexing Wives Bible (KJV, 1638)
Numbers 25:18 reads, "for they vex you with their wives" instead of "with their wiles."

Unrighteous Bible (KJV, Cambridge, 1653)
1 Corinthians 6:9, "the unrighteous shall not inherit the Kingdom of God" appears as "the unrighteous shall inherit the Kingdom of God."

PURSUIT

I fled Him, down the nights and down the days;
I fled Him, down the arches of the years;
I fled Him, down the labyrinthine ways
    Of my own mind; and in the mist of tears
I hid from Him, and under running laughter.
    Up vistaed hopes I sped;
    And shot, precipitated,
Adown Titanic glooms of chasmèd fears,
From those strong Feet that followed, followed after.
    But with unhurrying chase,
    And unperturbèd pace,

Deliberate speed, majestic instancy,
>   They beat—and a Voice beat
>   More instant than the Feet—
> "All things betray thee, who betrayest Me."

> —*opening lines of* The Hound of Heaven,
> *Francis Thompson (1859-1907), English poet*

SOME NAMES AND DESCRIPTIONS OF THE DEVIL

Abaddon (Rev. 9:11)—"angel of the bottomless pit"
adversary (1 Pet. 5:8)
angel of light (2 Cor. 11:14)
Apollyon (Rev. 9:11)
auld thief
Beelzebub, the prince of the devils (Matt. 12:24)
Belial (2 Cor. 6:15)
dragon—with seven heads, ten horns, and seven crowns (Rev. 12:3, 7, 9)
evil one (John 17:15)
father of lies (John 8:44)
foul fiend
god of this world (2 Cor. 4:4)
His Satanic Majesty
Lucifer (Isa. 14:12)
Mephistopheles
Old Clootie
old gentleman (in black)
Old Harry
Old Hornie
Old Nick
Old One
Old Scratchy
old serpent (Rev. 12:9; 20:2)

Prince of Darkness
prince of the power of the air (Eph. 2:2)
prince of this world (John 12:31; 14:30)
Satan (Job 1:6)
Tempter (1 Thess. 3:5)

PRAYER OF ST. FRANCIS

Sometimes known as the "Peace Prayer."

> Lord, make me an instrument of your peace.
> Where there is hatred, let me bring love.
> Where there is injury, pardon.
> Where there is discord, union.
> Where there is doubt, faith.
> Where there is despair, hope.
> Where there is darkness, light.
> Where there is sadness, joy.
>
> O Divine Master,
> grant that I may not so much seek to be consoled, as to console;
> to be understood, as to understand;
> to be loved, as to love;
> for it is in giving that we receive,
> it is in pardoning that we are pardoned,
> it is in dying that we are born to eternal life.

—although frequently attributed to Francis of Assisi, the earliest published version appeared only in 1912, in the French magazine La Clochette. *This English translation is a shortened version.*

CHARLEMAGNE'S RELICS

According to legend, when the emperor Charlemagne (c. 768–814) finished building Aachen Cathedral, he collected Christian relics from Rome, Constantinople, Jerusalem, and other Christian centers. Among them, preserved in the *Marienschrein* (Shrine of Mary), are the following:

> The Virgin Mary's cloak
> The infant Jesus's swaddling clothes
> The loincloth worn by Jesus on the cross
> The cloth in which John the Baptist's head was wrapped after his decapitation
> The cord used to bind Christ when he was flogged
> The Virgin Mary's girdle
> A piece of the sponge offered to Christ on the cross
> A lock of St. Bartholomew's hair
> Two of the apostle Thomas's teeth
> One of Simeon's arms
> A fragment of the cross
> A tooth of St. Catherine
> The point of a nail that fixed Christ to the cross
> A lock of John the Baptist's hair

"WHEN EARTH'S LAST PICTURE IS PAINTED"

> When Earth's last picture is painted and the tubes are twisted and dried,
> When the oldest colours have faded, and the youngest critic has died,
> We shall rest, and, faith, we shall need it—lie down for an aeon or two,
> Till the Master of All Good Workmen shall put us to work anew.

> And those that were good shall be happy: they shall sit in a golden chair;
> They shall splash at a ten-league canvas with brushes of comet's hair.
> They shall find real saints to draw from—Magdalene, Peter, and Paul;

They shall work for an age at a sitting and never be tired
   at all!

And only The Master shall praise us, and only The Master
   shall blame;
And no one shall work for money, and no one shall work
   for fame;
But each for the joy of the working, and each in his separate
   star,
Shall draw the Thing as he sees It for the God of Things as
   They are!

—Rudyard Kipling (1865-1936), English writer

BLESSINGS

The LORD bless thee, and keep thee:
The LORD make his face shine upon thee, and be gracious
   unto thee:
The LORD lift up his countenance upon thee, and give thee
   peace.

—Numbers 6:24-26

Now may the God and Father of our Lord Jesus Christ, and
the eternal high priest himself, the Son of God Jesus Christ,
build you up in faith and truth and in all gentleness and in all
freedom from anger and forbearance and steadfastness and
patient endurance and purity.

—Polycarp of Smyrna (69-156), Christian martyr

O Lord, support us all the day long of this troublous life,
until the shadows lengthen, and the evening comes,
and the busy world is hushed,
and the fever of life is over, and our work is done.
Then, Lord, in your mercy,

grant us a safe lodging, a holy rest,
and peace at the last.

> —*John Henry Newman (1801–1890),*
> *English theologian,*
> *based on a sixteenth-century prayer*

May the road rise up to meet you.
May the wind be always at your back.
May the sun shine warm upon your face; the rains fall
    softly on your fields and until we meet again,
May God hold you in the palm of his hand.

> —*Traditional Gaelic blessing*

THE FATE OF THE APOSTLES

Scripture does not record how any of the apostles, apart from John's brother James, died. However, tradition insists that all were martyred or banished as victims of Roman persecution. These dates, causes, and sites of death are derived from tradition, conjecture, and legend.

James, son of Zebedee ("James the Great/Greater")	First apostle to be martyred; beheaded by Herod Agrippa in Jerusalem, 44 CE. According to tradition, his remains are at Santiago de Compostela, Galicia, Spain.
Bartholomew	Crucified or flayed alive and beheaded at Albanopolis, Armenia, 52 CE
Andrew	Crucified on an X-shaped cross ("saltire") at Patras, Achaia, 60/70 CE
Matthew	Killed by the sword in Ethiopia, 60 CE
Barnabas	Stoned to death in Salamis, Cyprus, 61 CE
James, son of Alphaeus ("James the Less/Lesser")	Executed in Jerusalem, or crucified at Ostrakine, Lower Egypt, c. 62 CE

Peter	Crucified upside down in Rome, 64 CE
Jude (also known as Thaddeus)	Killed with an axe in Beirut, 65 CE
Paul	Beheaded in Rome, c. 66 CE
Thomas	Run through by a lance in India, 72 CE
Simon	Possibly sawn in half laterally at Suanir, Persia, 74 CE
Philip the Zealot/ Canaanite	Possibly crucified upside down in Phrygia, c. 80 CE
John	Author of the book of Revelation, by tradition the apostle John, son of Zebedee. Banished to the Isle of Patmos. Died Ephesus, c. 100 CE

And two gospel writers

Mark "the Evangelist"	Died after being dragged through the streets of Alexandria, 68 CE
Luke	Hanged from an olive tree in Thebes, Boeotia, 84 CE

A GRACE

> God of goodness, bless our food,
> Keep us in a pleasant mood.
> Bless the cook and all who serve us.
> From indigestion, Lord, preserve us.
>
> —*Anonymous*

SOME RELIGIOUS PLAYS

Timothy Dwight IV, president of Yale College from 1795 to 1817, declared, in his "Essay on the Stage" (1794): "To indulge a taste for playgoing means nothing more or less than the loss of that most valuable treasure: the immortal soul."

Following are some playwrights who didn't heed Dwight's warning:

Murder in the Cathedral, by T. S. Eliot (1935)
The Man Born to Be King, a radio drama by Dorothy L. Sayers (1941)
Becket, or The Honor of God, by Jean Anouilh (1959)
A Man for All Seasons, by Robert Bolt (1960)
Luther, by John Osborne (1961)
Racing Demon, by David Hare (1990)
Doubt: A Parable, by John Patrick Shanley (2004)
Anne Boleyn, by Howard Brenton (2010)
Written on the Heart—on the making of the King James Version—by David Edgar (2011)
York Mystery Plays—forty-eight mystery plays from creation through the last judgment

"TEMPTATION"

The billows swell, the winds are high,
Clouds overcast my wintry sky;
Out of the depths to Thee I call, —
My fears are great, my strength is small.

O Lord, the pilot's part perform,
And guard and guide me through the storm;
Defend me from each threatening ill,
Control the waves,—say, 'Peace! be still.'

Amidst the roaring of the sea
My soul still hangs her hope on Thee;
Thy constant love, thy faithful care,
Is all that saves me from despair.

> Though tempest toss'd and half a wreck,
> My Saviour through the storms I seek;
> Let neither wind nor stormy main
> Force back my shatter'd bark again.
>
> —*William Cowper (1731–1800)*

WHY "THE BIBLE"?

The word "Bible" is derived, through Latin, from the Greek *ta biblia*, meaning "the books." In Latin, *biblia* came to be understood as a single book. The Greek word *biblia* is derived from *biblos*, "papyrus." The earliest known use of *ta biblia* to mean "the Bible" comes in the Christian document 2 Clement, which contains a sermon written around the middle of the second century CE.

And "testament"? The word "testament" means "covenant." The Old Testament records several covenants between God and humankind, such as the covenant with Noah after the flood (Gen. 9:8–17); the covenant with Abraham (Gen. 15 and 17), promising that his descendants will possess the land of Canaan; and the covenant made with Moses and the Israelites at Mount Sinai (Exod. 19–24), after they escaped from slavery in Egypt. The New Testament records the new covenant between God and humankind, instituted by Jesus at the Last Supper.

ANYONE IN THE QUAD?

Catholic theologian Ronald Knox caricatures the philosophical position taken by George Berkeley (1685–1753): things exist only insofar as they are perceived.

> There once was a man who said "God
> Must think it exceedingly odd
> If he finds that this tree

Continues to be
When there's no one about in the Quad."

—Ronald Knox (1888-1957)

Anonymous response:

Dear Sir, Your astonishment's odd:
I am always about in the Quad.
And that's why the tree
Will continue to be,
Since observed by, Yours faithfully, God.

"PROFICISCERE"

A prayer of commendation when death seems near:

Go forward, Christian soul, in your journey from this world.
In the love of God the Father, who created you,
In the mercy of Jesus Christ, who suffered for you,
In the power of the Holy Spirit, who strengthens you,
In communion with the Saints,
sustained by Angels and Archangels,
and all the company of heaven.
May you dwell in peace.

*—ancient Christian prayer, paraphrase translation
from the Latin. For details, see John S. Lampard,*
Go Forth, Christian Soul: The Biography of a Prayer
(London: Epworth, 2005).

"THE BIBLE IS AN ANTIQUE VOLUME"

The Bible is an antique Volume—
Written by faded Men

At the suggestion of Holy Spectres—
Subjects—Bethlehem—
Eden—the ancient Homestead—
Satan—the Brigadier—
Judas—the Great Defaulter—
David—the Troubadour—
Sin—a distinguished Precipice
Others must resist—
Boys that "believe" are very lonesome—
Other Boys are "lost"—
Had but the Tale a warbling Teller—
All the Boys would come—
Orpheus' Sermon captivated—
It did not condemn—

—*Emily Dickinson (1830-1886), American poet*

BIBLICAL RECORDS

The Bible's longest and shortest (all according to the King James Version):

Shortest reign: Zimri ruled Israel for seven days, then committed suicide by burning his palace around him (1 Kings 16:15).
Longest reign: Manasseh started to reign when he was twelve, and ruled Judah for fifty-five years (2 Kings 21:1).
Youngest king: Joash (a.k.a. Jehoash) was seven when he became king of Judah, and reigned for forty years (2 Chron. 24:1).
Biggest army: Zerah the Ethiopian reportedly had an army of one million (a thousand thousand), which he ranged against King Asa (2 Chron. 14:9).
Longest Old Testament book: Psalms—150 chapters and 2,461 verses. Psalms is also the longest book in the entire Bible.
Shortest book in the Old Testament: Obadiah—21 verses and a mere 670 words.
Shortest book in the New Testament: 2 John—13 verses and only 298 words.

Longest chapter in the Bible: Psalm 119—176 verses.

Shortest chapter in the Bible: Psalm 117—2 verses and a mere 33 words.

The two shortest Bible verses: "Eber, Peleg, Reu" (1 Chron. 1:25) and "Jesus wept" (John 11:35).

Longest verse in the Bible: Esther 8:9—90 words.

Total number of verses in the Bible: 30,442; Old Testament: 22,485; New Testament: 7,957.

Oddest verse in the Bible?: "At Parbar westward, four at the causeway, and two at Parbar" (1 Chron. 26:18).

Longest name in the Bible: Maher-shalal-hash-baz (Isa. 8:1, 3)—the prophet Isaiah's son.

Shortest prayer in the Bible: "Lord, save me" (Matt. 14:30), cried by Peter, terrified while walking on Lake Galilee.

ON MARRIAGE

What greater thing is there for two human souls than to feel that they are joined for life, to strengthen each other in all labor, to rest on each other in all sorrow, to minister to each other in all pain, to be one with each other in silent unspeakable memories of the moment of the last parting?

—*George Eliot (Mary Ann Evans, 1819–1880),*
English novelist

JOHN WESLEY'S ADVICE TO PREACHERS

Wesley traveled some 250,000 miles in his mission to evangelize the British Isles. This is the advice he offered other preachers:

i. Invite
ii. Convince
iii. Offer Christ
iv. Build up—to some degree in every sermon.

1. Be sure to begin and end precisely at the time appointed.
2. Endeavor to be serious, weighty, and solemn in your deportment before the congregation.
3. Always suit your subject to the audience.
4. Choose the plainest texts you can.
5. Take care not to ramble from your text.
6. Beware of too much allegorizing or spiritualizing.
7. Beware of anything awkward or affected, in your phrase, gesture, or pronunciation.

A PILGRIM'S PRAYER

Give me my scallop shell of quiet,
    My staff of faith to walk upon,
My scrip of joy, immortal diet,
    My bottle of salvation,
My gown of glory, hope's true gage;
And thus I'll take my pilgrimage.

—from "The Passionate Man's Pilgrimage,"
Walter Raleigh (1552–1618), English explorer and poet

WHO ARE THE GIDEONS?

If you've ever slept in a hotel, you will have found a Gideon Bible by your bedside.

The Gideons International is an organization of Christian businessmen that distributes Bibles and New Testaments to hotels, schools, hospitals, and prisons, and to members of the armed forces and police officers and firefighters.

The Gideons were set up in the United States in 1899 by three Christian commercial travelers: John H. Nicholson, Samuel E. Hill, and Will J. Knights. They named themselves "Gideons" after the Israelite leader Gideon (Judg. 7), who won a great battle with a select few warriors. In 1908, they decided to place a Bible in the bedroom of every American hotel.

The first twenty-five were left at the Superior Hotel, Iron Mountain, Montana.

The Gideons spread to Canada in 1911, and to the United Kingdom in 1949, and are today a worldwide organization.

WHEN WAS THE WORLD CREATED?

Archbishop James Ussher (1581–1656) calculated that the first day of creation was Sunday, October 2, 4004 BCE, and that God finished creating the world the following Saturday.

Ussher then worked out that Adam and Eve were expelled from Eden on Monday, November 10, 4004 BCE, and that Noah's ark came to rest on Mount Ararat on Wednesday, May 5, 1491 BCE.

However, the French scholar Joseph Scaliger (1540–1609) dated creation to 3950 BCE, while the Jewish calendar dates it as recent as October 3761 BCE.

THE SHEPHERD

> He is not drowning his sheep when he washeth them, nor killing them when he is shearing them. But by this he showeth that they are his own; and the new shorn sheep do most visibly bear his name or mark, when it is almost worn out and scarce discernible on them that have the longest fleece.
>
> —*Richard Baxter (1615–1691), English Puritan*

"THE DONKEY"

> When fishes flew and forests walked
>   And figs grew upon thorn,

Some moment when the moon was blood
>   Then surely I was born.

With monstrous head and sickening cry
>   And ears like errant wings,
The devil's walking parody
>   On all four-footed things.

The tattered outlaw of the earth,
>   Of ancient crooked will;
Starve, scourge, deride me: I am dumb,
>   I keep my secret still.

Fools! For I also had my hour;
>   One far fierce hour and sweet:
There was a shout about my ears,
>   And palms before my feet.

>   —G. K. Chesterton (1874–1936), *English author*

A WELSH VILLAGE BAPTISM

When I got to the chapel my beard moustache and whiskers were so stiff with ice that I could hardly open my mouth and my beard was frozen on to my mackintosh. There was a large christening party from Llwyn Gwilym. The baby was baptized in ice which was broken and swimming about in the font.

>   —Rev. Francis Kilvert (1840–1879), *English clergyman,
>   diary entry for February 13, 1870*

PARSONS PECULIAR

The Anglican Church has attracted some notably eccentric clergymen.

Archbishop George Abbot (1562-1633), known to be a poor marksman, accidentally killed a gamekeeper during a hunting party.

Rev. Thomas Hunter was executed in August 1700, having murdered two children who discovered his affair with a maid. He declared on the scaffold, "There is no God, or if there be, I hold him in defiance."

While based in Nevis, in the West Indies, *Rev. Lancelot Blackburne* (1658-1743) is reputed to have sailed with a pirate ship, claiming his share of the booty. He was later appointed archbishop of York, while maintaining his "reputation for carnality."

Rev. Edward Stokes (1706-1798), blind rector of Blaby, Leicestershire, rode to hounds, accompanied by a groom who rang a bell when he needed to jump a hedge.

Frederick Augustus Hervey (1730-1803), when bishop of Derry, arranged a curates' race on the beach, rewarding winners with church appointments.

Rev. Augustus Toplady (1740-1778), author of the hymn "Rock of Ages," calculated that every human being commits 630,720,000 sins before attaining the age of thirty.

Henry Bate (1745-1824), rector of North Fambridge, Essex, fought five duels, edited two muckraking papers, and was co-respondent in a celebrated adultery trial.

Rev. John ("Jack") Russell (1795-1883), the "sporting parson," famous as a boxer and wrestler, developed a pack of fox terriers that were named after him.

DARWIN'S DENIAL

Charles Darwin (1809-1882), author of *The Origin of Species*, was normally reluctant to discuss his views on religion, for fear of hurting the feelings of his family. But there was one notable exception: in 1880, in response to a letter from one Frederick McDermott, seeking confirmation of Darwin's faith before he read his books, Darwin wrote:

DOWN,
BECKENHAM, KENT.

Private
Dear Sir

I am sorry to have to inform you that I do not believe in the Bible as a divine revelation, & therefore not in Jesus Christ as the son of God.

yours faithfully
Ch. Darwin

ON SLAVERY

An excellent law might be made out of the Pennsylvania one for the gradual abolition of slavery. Till America comes into this Measure her Prayers to Heaven for Liberty will be impious. This is a strong expression but it is Just.

—John Jay (1745–1829), first chief justice
of the United States, letter to Egbert Benson,
September 18, 1780

I love the pure, peaceable, and impartial Christianity of Christ: I therefore hate the corrupt, slaveholding, women-whipping, cradle-plundering, partial and hypocritical Christianity of this land.

—Frederick Douglass (1818–1895),
American abolitionist

LOVE AND TRUTH

Truth and Love are wings that cannot be separated, for Truth without Love is unable to fly, so too Love without Truth is unable to soar upward: their yoke is one harmony.

—from Hymns on Faith, *Ephrem of Syria (306–373),*
churchman and writer

There is nothing that makes us love someone so much as praying for them.

—*William Law (1686-1761), English writer*

It is harder for some people to believe that God loves them than to believe that he exists.

—*Cardinal Basil Hume (1923-1999),*
English Catholic churchman

The Christian does not think God will love us because we are good, but that God will make us good because he loves us.

—*C. S. Lewis (1898-1963), English writer*

DOES THE BIBLE REALLY SAY THAT?

It's commonly said that "Money is the root of all evil"; however, the Bible actually says, "the love of money is the root of all evil" (1 Tim. 6:10).

It's often said that Esau sold his birthright to his brother for a "mess of pottage"; however, the words "mess of" do not appear in the King James Bible (Gen. 25:30-34): only "red pottage" and "pottage of lentils."

People often assume the phrase "Go the way of all flesh" is from Scripture; in fact, the King James Version says "going the way of all the earth" (Josh. 23:14).

It's commonly said that, after Elijah prayed for fire from heaven, he saw "a cloud no bigger than a man's hand." The King James Version reads: "Behold, there ariseth a little cloud out of the sea, like a man's hand" (1 Kings 18:44).

The phrase "The lion shall lie down with the lamb" is frequently quoted as if verbatim from Scripture. In fact, the King James Version reads: "The wolf also shall dwell with the lamb, and the leopard shall lie down with the kid; and the calf and the young lion and the fatling together; and a little child shall lead them" (Isa. 11:6).

LITURGY FOR DOUBTERS

O God, forasmuch as without Thee
We are not enabled to doubt Thee,
Help us all by Thy grace
To convince the whole race
It knows nothing whatever about Thee.

—*Ronald Knox (1888–1957), English theologian*

HYMN FOR THE LAST CHURCH OF ALL

We know Thee not nor guess Thee,
   O vague beyond our dreams,
We praise Thee not nor bless Thee,
   Dim source of all that seems.
Unconscious be our witness,
   The music of the heart,
O It becomes all Itness
   If aught indeed Thou art.

—*Terrot Reaveley Glover (1869–1943),*
Cambridge lecturer

THE APOSTLE PAUL

A man of little stature, thin-haired upon the head, crooked in the legs, of good state of body, with eyebrows joining and a nose somewhat crooked; full of grace, for sometimes he appeared like a man, and sometimes had the face of an angel.

—*Acts of Paul and Thecla, late second century CE*

WORDS OF THE MARTYRS

The blood of the martyrs is the seed of the church.

—*attributed to Tertullian (160–225), church father*

A more faithful translation might run:

> "The more you mow us down the more we multiply: the blood of Christians is seed."

> Then, the proconsul urging him, and saying, "Swear, and I will set thee at liberty, reproach Christ"; Polycarp declared, "Eighty and six years have I served Him, and He never did me any injury: how then can I blaspheme my King and my Saviour?"

> —*from Martyrdom of Polycarp; Polycarp (69–155) was eighty-six or eighty-seven when he died*

> He is no fool who gives what he cannot keep to gain what he cannot lose.

> —*Jim Elliot (1927–1956), American missionary, killed in Ecuador, 1956*

FOR WHOM THE BELL TOLLS

> No man is an island, entire of itself; every man is a piece of the continent, a part of the main. If a clod be washed away by the sea, Europe is the less, as well as if a promontory were, as well as if a manor of thy friend's or of thine own were: any man's death diminishes me, because I am involved in mankind, and therefore never send to know for whom the bell tolls; it tolls for thee.

> —*John Donne (1572–1631), English writer*

ESSENTIAL BIBLE MANUSCRIPTS

There are more copies of the New Testament than any other document in ancient history.

We possess more than 6,000 manuscript copies of either the entire Greek New Testament or parts of it. By contrast, we have only about 650 manuscript copies of Homer's *Iliad*, and these date from 200 to 300 CE, more than a thousand years after it was composed. There are just 9 good extant copies of Caesar's *Gallic Wars* and 8 manuscripts of Herodotus's *History*.

The three oldest and most important extant Greek manuscripts of the Bible are:

Codex Vaticanus
Dating to c. 350 CE, this manuscript contains the entire Bible and Septuagint, except Genesis 1–46, Psalms 105–137, and the New Testament after Hebrews 9:14. Housed in the Vatican Library, Rome.

Codex Sinaiticus
Dating to early in the fourth century, this manuscript, discovered at St. Catherine's Monastery, Sinai, in the nineteenth century, contains the entire New Testament except for twenty-four verses, but only 145 leaves of the Septuagint—roughly half the Old Testament. Housed in the British Library, London.

Codex Alexandrinus
Dating to the early fifth century, this contains the entire New Testament, save thirty-four chapters (mainly Matthew), and the entire Septuagint, except 10 leaves. Housed in the British Library, London.

ON UNDERSTANDING SCRIPTURE

When thou dost take this sacred book into thy hand
Think not that thou the included sense dost understand.

It is a sign thou wantest sound intelligence
If that thou think thyself to understand the sense.

Be not deceived thou then on it in vain mayst gaze;
The way is intricate that leads into a maze.

Here's naught but what's mysterious to an understanding
   eye
Where reverence alone stands ope, and sense stands by.

—*Thomas Traherne (1636/37-1674), English writer*

PROPHETS

I do not feel obliged to believe that the same God who has endowed us with sense, reason, and intellect has intended us to forgo their use.

—*Galileo Galilei (1564-1642), Italian scientist*

If a man does not keep pace with his companions, perhaps it is because he hears a different drummer. Let him step to the music which he hears, however measured or far away.

—*from* Walden, *Henry David Thoreau (1817-1862), American philosopher*

When I give food to the poor, they call me a saint. When I ask why the poor have no food, they call me a communist.

—*Dom Hélder Câmara (1909-1999), Brazilian archbishop*

STIRRING LAST WORDS

Hagiography may have contributed to the following valedictions:

Lord, lay not this sin to their charge. (Acts 7:60)
—*Stephen, the first Christian martyr, c. 34 CE*

Turn me! I am roasted on one side.
—*St. Lawrence, martyred on a heated gridiron, 258 CE*

Welcome, Sister Death!
—*Francis of Assisi, Italian saint, 1230*

Be of good comfort, Master Ridley, and play the man! We shall this day light such a candle, by God's grace, in England as I trust shall never be put out.

> —*Bishop Hugh Latimer to his friend Bishop Nicholas Ridley as they were burnt at the stake in Oxford for their Protestant beliefs, 1555*

I go from a corruptible to an incorruptible crown, where no disturbance can be, no disturbance in the world.

> —*King Charles I, executed at Whitehall, London, 1649*

My design is to make what haste I can to be gone.

> —*Lord Protector Oliver Cromwell, 1658*

The best of all is, God is with us. Farewell! Farewell!

> —*John Wesley, English evangelist, 1791*

I have lived as a philosopher and I die as a Christian.

> —*Giacomo Casanova, notorious Italian libertine, 1798*

I go with the gladness of a boy bounding away from school. I feel so strong in Christ.

> —*Adoniram Judson, American Baptist missionary to Myanmar, 1850*

Let us cross over the river and rest under the shade of the trees!

> —*Thomas "Stonewall" Jackson, American Confederate general, 1863*

This is my triumph; this is my coronation day. It is glorious!

> —*Dwight L. Moody, American evangelist, 1899*

TROUBLES

I compare the troubles which we have to undergo in the course of the year to a great bundle of faggots, far too large for us to lift. But God does not require us to carry the whole at once. He mercifully unties the bundle, and gives us first one stick, which we are to carry today, and then another, which we are to carry tomorrow, and so on. This we might easily manage, if we would only take the burden appointed for each day; but we choose to increase our troubles by carrying yesterday's stick over again today, and adding tomorrow's burden to the load, before we are required to bear it.

—*John Newton (1725–1807), English hymn writer*

Worry does not empty tomorrow of its sorrow; it empties today of its strength.

—*Corrie ten Boom (1892–1983),*
concentration camp survivor

I know God will not give me anything I can't handle. I just wish that he didn't trust me so much.

—*Mother Teresa of Calcutta (1910–1997),*
Roman Catholic nun and missionary

MORE WORDS ON THE GOOD BOOK

Thy word is a lamp unto my feet, and a light unto my path.

—*Psalm 119:105*

Search the scriptures; for in them ye think ye have eternal life.

—*John 5:39*

The Bible is a book that has been read more and examined less than any book that ever existed.

—*Thomas Paine (1737–1809), American revolutionary*

The English Bible, a book which, if everything else in our language should perish, would alone suffice to show the whole extent of its beauty and power.

—*Lord Macaulay (1800–1859), English historian*

Bible reading is an education in itself.

> —*Alfred, Lord Tennyson (1809–1892), English poet*

Holy Scripture containeth all things necessary to salvation.

> —*Book of Common Prayer, 1562*

But no public man in these islands ever believes that the Bible means what it says: he is always convinced that it says what he means.

> —*George Bernard Shaw (1856–1950),*
> *English playwright*

The Bible is to me the most precious thing in the world just because it tells me the story of Jesus.

> —*George Macdonald (1842–1905), Scottish author*

AVE MARIA GRATIA PLENA

Was this his coming! I had hoped to see
A scene of wondrous glory, as was told
Of some great God who in a rain of gold
Broke open bars and fell on Danae:
Or a dread vision as when Semele,
Sickening for love and unappeased desire,
Prayed to see God's clear body, and the fire
Caught her brown limbs and slew her utterly.
With such glad dreams I sought this holy place,
And now with wondering eyes and heart I stand
Before this supreme mystery of Love:
Some kneeling girl with passionless pale face,
An angel with a lily in his hand,
And over both the white wings of a Dove.

> —*Oscar Wilde (1854–1900), Irish playwright*

ADAM AND EVE

What time of day was Adam created?
A little before Eve.

How do we know Adam was a great athlete?
He came first in the human race.

How did Adam and Eve feel about God expelling them from Eden?
They were really put out.

How did Adam and Eve react to being ejected from the garden?
They raised Cain.

SOME SCARY THEOLOGICAL TERMS

Adiaphora: Theological points that don't directly affect salvation or aren't specifically discussed in the Bible.

Dispensationalism: A system that divides Bible history into periods during which God relates to the course of events in a different way.

Fideism: The doctrine that knowledge of divine matters can be attained by faith alone, not through the intellect.

Infralapsarianism: A view of predestination which holds that God's decrees as to who would be the elect occurred after the fall of man; contrasts with supralapsarianism.

Latitudinarianism: Retaining conventional church practices while de-emphasizing dogma, church organization, and worship.

Perichōrēsis: Any characteristic or action attributed to one person of the Trinity should also be attributed to the other two.

Supralapsarianism: Calvinist doctrine that, before the fall of Adam and Eve, God chose those who would be saved and those who would be damned.

Transubstantiation: Roman Catholic doctrine that the bread and wine of the Mass, when consecrated, miraculously become the physical body and blood of Jesus.

Trichotomism: The idea that human beings are a unity of three separate parts: body, soul, and spirit.

SCRIPTURE UNAWARES

Old Testament phrases in the King James Version that have become commonplace:

My brother's keeper (Gen. 4:9)
There were giants in the earth in those days (Gen. 6:4)
Milk and honey (Exod. 3:8)
Flesh pots (Exod. 16:3)
Apple of his eye (Deut. 32:10)
A man after his own heart (1 Sam. 13:14)
How are the mighty fallen! (2 Sam. 1:19)
A still small voice (1 Kings 19:12)
The skin of my teeth (Job 19:20)
The root of the matter (Job 19:28)
Out of the mouth of babes and sucklings (Ps. 8:2)
Beat their swords into plowshares (Isa. 2:4)
Be horribly afraid (Jer. 2:12)
Let us now praise famous men (Sir. 44:1)

"PIED BEAUTY"

Glory be to God for dappled things—
    For skies of couple-color as a brinded cow;
        For rose-moles all in stipple upon trout that swim;
Fresh-firecoal chestnut-falls; finches' wings;
    Landscape plotted and pieced—fold, fallow, and plough;
        And áll trádes, their gear and tackle and trim.

All things counter, original, spare, strange;
>   Whatever is fickle, freckled (who knows how?)
>> With swift, slow; sweet, sour; adazzle, dim;
>
> He fathers-forth whose beauty is past change:
> Praise him.

—*Gerard Manley Hopkins (1844–1889), English poet*

THE APOSTLES' CREED

The landmark fourth-century statement of faith is as follows:

> I believe in God the Father Almighty, Maker of heaven and earth.
>
> And in Jesus Christ, his only Son our Lord, who was conceived by the Holy Spirit, born of the Virgin Mary, suffered under Pontius Pilate, was crucified, dead, and buried; he descended into hell; the third day he rose again from the dead; he ascended into heaven; and sitteth on the right hand of God the Father Almighty; from thence he shall come to judge the quick and the dead.
>
> I believe in the Holy Spirit, the holy catholic Church, the communion of saints, the forgiveness of sins, the resurrection of the body and the life everlasting.

JESUS'S SEVEN LAST WORDS FROM THE CROSS

The Gospels record seven statements Jesus made while dying on the cross. Since they are recorded by different writers, they can't be organized chronologically.

> "Father, forgive them; for they know not what they do" (Luke 23:34), referring to those crucifying Jesus.

> "To-day shalt thou be with me in paradise" (Luke 23:43), to the penitent thief crucified next to Jesus.

"Woman, behold thy son! . . . Behold thy mother!" (John 19:26, 27). Jesus to his mother, Mary, and to his disciple John.

"Eli, Eli, lama sabachthani?" Aramaic for "My God, my God, why hast thou forsaken me?" (Matt. 27:46; Mark 15:34, quoting Ps. 22:1).

"I thirst" (John 19:28), probably referencing Psalm 69:21: "in my thirst they gave me vinegar to drink."

"Father, into thy hands I commend my spirit" (Luke 23:46), referring to Psalm 31:5, "Into thine hand I commit my spirit."

"It is finished" (John 19:30).

"LOVE DIVINE"

An enduringly popular hymn, frequently sung at weddings.

> Love divine, all loves excelling,
> Joy of heaven to earth come down;
> Fix in us thy humble dwelling;
> All thy faithful mercies crown.
> Jesus, thou art all compassion,
> Pure, unbounded love thou art;
> Visit us with thy salvation,
> Enter every trembling heart.
>
> Come, almighty to deliver,
> Let us all thy grace receive;
> Suddenly return, and never,
> Never more thy temples leave.
> Thee we would be always blessing,
> Serve thee as thy hosts above,

Pray and praise thee without ceasing,
Glory in thy perfect love.

Finish then thy new creation:
Pure and spotless let us be;
Let us see thy great salvation
Perfectly restored in thee;
Changed from glory into glory,
Till in heaven we take our place,
Till we cast our crowns before thee,
Lost in wonder, love, and praise.

Charles Wesley (1707-1788), English hymn writer

ONE SOLITARY LIFE

He was born in an obscure village, the child of a peasant woman. He worked in a carpentry shop until he was thirty, and then for three years he was an itinerant preacher. When the tide of popular opinion turned against him, his friends ran away. He was turned over to his enemies. He was tried and convicted. He was nailed upon a cross between two thieves. When he was dead, he was laid in a borrowed grave. He never wrote a book. He never held an office. He never owned a home. He never went to college. He never traveled more than two hundred miles from the place where he was born. He never did any of the things that usually accompany greatness. Yet all the armies that ever marched, and all the governments that have ever sat, and all the kings that ever reigned have not affected life upon this earth as powerfully as has that One Solitary Life.

—possibly based on an essay by Dr. James Allan Francis (1864-1928), an American pastor

SOME CLASSICS OF SPIRITUALITY

Julian of Norwich: *Revelations of Divine Love*
Thomas à Kempis: *The Imitation of Christ*
Thomas Traherne: *Centuries of Meditations*
St. Teresa of Avila: *Interior Castle*
Brother Lawrence: *The Practice of the Presence of God*
Pope John XXIII: *Journal of a Soul*
Francis De Sales: *The Complete Introduction to the Devout Life*
Thomas Merton: *The Seven Storey Mountain*
Henri J. M. Nouwen: *The Return of the Prodigal Son*

THE POPE IS DEAD

Some twenty-six popes are believed to have been assassinated. They include:

John VIII (r. 872–882)	poisoned, then clubbed to death
Stephen VI (r. 896–897)	strangled
John X (r. 914–928)	possibly suffocated with a pillow
Stephen VIII (or IX) (r. 939–942)	so badly mutilated that he died of his injuries
John XII (r. 955–964)	said to have been murdered by "an outraged husband"
Benedict VI (r. 973–974)	strangled by a priest
John XIV (r. 983–984)	starved or poisoned
Gregory V (r. 996–999)	rumored to have been poisoned—though possibly died of malaria

THE FOUR EVANGELISTS AND THEIR SYMBOLS

Each of the four gospel writers has a distinctive icon, frequently depicted in sculpture, carving, and stained glass.

Matthew: Winged man or angel
Mark: Winged lion
Luke: Winged ox or bull
John: Eagle

These symbols originate from the four "living creatures" drawing the throne-chariot of God, the *Merkabah*, mentioned in Ezekiel 1 and Revelation 4:6-9.

COMMON PHRASES FROM THE PRAYER BOOK

The Episcopal *Book of Common Prayer* has contributed many resonant phrases to everyday English.

The world, the flesh, and the devil.

—Litany

In the midst of life we are in death.

—*from the Latin* Media vita in morte sumus,
first line of a fourteenth-century Gregorian chant

Earth to earth, ashes to ashes.

—*from the* Order for Burial of the Dead

Read, mark, learn, and inwardly digest.

—Collect for the 2nd Sunday in Advent

If any man can shew any just cause, why they may not lawfully be joined together, let him now speak, or else hereafter for ever hold his peace.

—*from* Solemnization of Matrimony

Till death us do part.

—*from* Solemnization of Matrimony

ANTI-SEMITISM CHALLENGED

How odd
of God
To choose
the Jews

*—William Norman Ewer, "Trilby" (1885–1976),
British journalist and Soviet spy*

But not so odd
As those who choose
A Jewish God,
But spurn the Jews.

*—attributed to Cecil Browne (1932–) or
Ogden Nash (1902–1971), American poet*

PRAYER OF ST. COLUMBA

Be thou a bright flame before me,
Be thou a guiding star above me,
Be thou a smooth path below me,
Be thou a kindly shepherd behind me,
Today, tonight, and for ever.

—Columba (521–597), Irish missionary monk

NAMES OF GOD

O Thou who art! Ecclesiastes names thee the Almighty; the Maccabees name thee Creator; the epistle to the Ephesians names thee Liberty . . . the Psalms name thee Wisdom and Truth; John names thee Light; the Book of Kings names thee Lord; Exodus calls thee Providence; Leviticus, Holiness; Esdras, Justice; creation calls thee God; man names thee Father; but Solomon names thee Compassion, which is the most beautiful of all thy names.

> *—from* Les Miserables,
> *Victor Hugo (1802–1885), French novelist*

LIKE CHRIST

I expect to pass through this life but once. If therefore there be any kindness I can show, or any good thing that I can do to any fellow being, let me do it now, and not defer or neglect it, as I shall not pass this way again.

> *—attributed to William Penn (1644–1718),*
> *Quaker, founder of Pennsylvania*

Though I am not what I ought to be, nor what I wish to be, nor what I hope to be, I can truly say, I am not what I once was . . . and I can heartily join with the apostle, and acknowledge, "By the grace of God I am what I am."

> *—John Newton (1725–1807), English hymn writer*

Being a Christian is more than just an instantaneous conversion—it is a daily process whereby you grow to be more and more like Christ.

> *—Billy Graham (1918–2018), American evangelist*

Christ literally walked in our shoes.

> *—Tim Keller (1950–), American pastor*

JESUS SOIT EN MA TESTE

God be in my head,
And in my understanding;
God be in my eyes,

And in my looking;
God be in my mouth,
And in my speaking;
God be in my heart,
And in my thinking;
God be at my end,
And at my departing.

> *—Old Sarum Primer and* Pynson's Horae, *1514, from a French prayer, c. 1490. There is a fine choral setting by Walford Davies (1869–1941).*

MAJOR JEWISH FESTIVALS

Jewish New Year (*Rosh Hashanah*) on 1 Tishri (early September). Ram's-horn trumpets, or *shofars*, are sounded during religious services.

The Day of Atonement (*Yom Kippur*) on 10 Tishri (mid to late September or early October) is the most solemn annual day of prayer, fasting, and repentance for sins.

The Feast of Ingathering, Tabernacles, or Booths (Hebrew *Sukkot*) is a thanksgiving festival held on 15–21 Tishri (late September or early October). Shelters, booths, or "tabernacles" are constructed, recalling the tents in which the Hebrews lived in the Sinai Desert, after having escaped slavery in Egypt.

Hanukkah (or *Chanuka*), the Feast of Dedication, or Lights, celebrated on 25–30 Kislev (mid to late December), to remember the recapture and cleansing of the Jerusalem temple by Judas Maccabaeus in 164 BCE, following its desecration by Antiochus Epiphanes.

Purim, the Feast of Lots, is celebrated on 14 or 15 Adar (late February) and commemorates the deliverance of the Persian Jews from a plot to have them massacred, recounted in the book of Esther.

The Feast of Unleavened Bread, or Passover (Hebrew *Pesach*), commemorates the Hebrews' escape from slavery in Egypt and begins on 14 Nissan (late March or early April) in the Jewish calendar. Unleavened bread is eaten for seven days.

The Feast of Harvest, also known as the Feast of Weeks and Day of First Fruits (Hebrew *Shavuot*), was a harvest festival but also commemorates the giving of the law to Moses at Mount Sinai. It is celebrated on 6 Sivan (mid to late May). Since it occurs on the fiftieth day after Passover, it is also known as Pentecost (Greek *pentekoste*, "fiftieth").

9 Av (Hebrew *Tisha B'Av*) is a day of prayer and fasting to remember the destruction of Solomon's temple by the Babylonians in 586 BCE, and of the Second Temple by the Romans in 70 CE. Celebrated on the 9 Av (mid to late July).

FINISHING

O Lord God, when thou givest to thy servants to endeavour any great matter, grant us also to know that it is not the beginning, but the continuing of the same unto the end, until it be thoroughly finished, which yieldeth the true glory; through him who for the finishing of thy work laid down his life, our Redeemer, Jesus Christ.

—*Prayer attributed to Sir Francis Drake (1541–1596),*
English admiral

TEN SACRED MUSIC MASTERWORKS

Giovanni Palestrina: *Missa Papae Marcelli*
Claudio Monteverdi: *Vespers*
J. S. Bach: *St. Matthew Passion*
Georg Frideric Handel: *Messiah*
Josef Haydn: *The Creation*
W. A. Mozart: *Requiem*
Ludwig van Beethoven: *Missa Solemnis*
Giuseppe Verdi: *Requiem*
Johannes Brahms: *German Requiem*
Benjamin Britten: *War Requiem*

FAITH AND WORKS

Expect great things from God;
Attempt great things for God.

>—William Carey (1761-1834),
>pioneer Baptist missionary

Work as if everything depended upon your work,
and pray as if everything depended upon your prayer.

>—William Booth (1829-1912),
>founder of the Salvation Army

The whole doctrine of justification by faith hinges, for me, upon my painfully reluctant realization that my Father is not going to be any more pleased with me when I am good than he is now when I am bad. He accepts me and delights in me as I am. It is ridiculous of him, but that is how it is between us.

>—John V. Taylor (1914-2001), bishop of Winchester

The basic premise of religion—that if you live a good life, things will go well for you—is wrong. Jesus was the most morally upright person who ever lived, yet he had a life filled with the experience of poverty, rejection, injustice, and even torture.

>—Tim Keller (1950-), American pastor

SOME WRITERS' EPITAPHS

Reader, I am to let thee know,
Donne's body only lies below;
For could the grave his soul comprise,
Earth would be richer than the skies.

>—John Donne (1572-1631), St. Paul's Cathedral, London

The body of Benjamin Franklin, Printer,
Like the cover of an old book
Its contents worn out,
And stripped of its lettering and gilding,
Lies here, food for worms.
Yet the work shall not be lost,
For it will (as he believed) appear once more,
In a new and most beautiful Edition,
corrected and amended
By the Author.

> —*Benjamin Franklin (1706-1790),*
> *found among his papers but not on his tombstone*

Called Back.

> —*Emily Dickinson (1830-1886),*
> *Amherst, Massachusetts*

Here the whole world (stars, water, air,
And field, and forest, as they were
Reflected in a single mind)
Like cast off clothes was left behind
In ashes, yet with hopes that she,
Re-born from holy poverty,
In lenten lands, hereafter may
Resume them on her Easter Day.

> —*For Joy Davidman (1915-1960), by her husband,*
> *C. S. Lewis, Headington Quarry, Oxford*

TEN STRONG THINGS

There are ten strong things.
Iron is strong, but fire melts it.
Fire is strong, but water quenches it.
Water is strong, but the clouds evaporate it.

Clouds are strong, but wind drives them away.
People are strong, but fears cast them down.
Fear is strong, but sleep overcomes it.
Sleep is strong, yet death is stronger.
But loving kindness survives death.

—The Talmud (adapted)

SOME CHRISTIAN CLASSICS

Augustine: *Confessions*
Thomas Aquinas: *Summa Theologica*
Blaise Pascal: *Pensées*
Karl Barth: *Church Dogmatics*
H. Richard Niebuhr: *Christ and Culture*
Dietrich Bonhoeffer: *Letters and Papers from Prison*
Gustavo Gutiérrez: *A Theology of Liberation*
Søren Kierkegaard: *Fear and Trembling*
G. K. Chesterton: *Orthodoxy*
Hans Küng: *On Being a Christian*
Paul Tillich: *The Courage to Be*
John Hick: *Evil and the God of Love*

"TIME IS"

Too Slow for those who Wait,
Too Swift for those who Fear,
Too Long for those who Grieve,
Too Short for those who Rejoice;
But for those who Love,
Time is not.

—from Music and Other Poems,
Henry van Dyke Jr. (1852–1933), American author

SOJOURNERS

An outsider observes second-century Christians:

> They dwell in their own countries but simply as sojourners. As citizens, they share in all things with others, and yet endure all slings as if foreigners. Every foreign land is to them as their native country, and every land of their birth as a land of strangers. They marry, as do others; they beget children; but they do not destroy their offspring. They have a common table but not a common bed. They are in the flesh, but they do not live after the flesh. They pass their days on earth, but are citizens of heaven. They obey the prescribed laws, and at the same time surpass the laws in their lives. They love all, and are persecuted by all. . . . They are poor, yet they make many rich. They are completely destitute, and yet they enjoy complete abundance. . . . They are reviled, and yet they bless. . . . When they do good they are punished as evildoers; undergoing punishment, they rejoice because they are brought to life.
>
> —Epistle to Diognetus, *c. 130 CE*

ICONIC PAINTINGS

- *The Annunciation*, Fra Angelico, painted c. 1440–1445: Convent of San Marco, Florence
- *The Baptism of Christ*, Piero della Francesca, c. 1448–1450: National Gallery, London
- *The Last Supper* (*Il Cenacolo*), Leonardo da Vinci, 1495–1498: Convent of Santa Maria delle Grazie, Milan
- *Creation of Adam*, Michelangelo, 1508–1512: Sistine Chapel, Rome
- *Madonna dell Granduca*, Raphael, 1506–1507: Uffizi Gallery, Florence

Isenheim Altarpiece, Grünewald, 1516: Unterlinden Museum, Colmar, France

Supper at Emmaus, Caravaggio, 1601: National Gallery, London

The Descent from the Cross, Rubens, 1612–1614: Cathedral of our Lady, Antwerp

The Return of the Prodigal Son, Rembrandt, 1663–1669: The Hermitage, St. Petersburg

Christ on the Cross, Velazquez, c. 1632: Prado, Madrid

The Light of the World, Holman Hunt, 1851–1853: Keble College, Oxford

Christ of Saint John of the Cross, Salvador Dali, 1951: Kelvingrove Art Gallery, Glasgow

A VILLAIN PASSES

At last, with a final struggle, the villain has passed away. Observing his malice increase daily, injuring the body of the church, the Governor of our souls has lopped him off like a cancer. His departure delights the survivors, but possibly dismays the dead; there is fear that, provoked by his company, they may send him back to us. Therefore care must be taken to order the Guild of Undertakers to place a very large, heavy stone on his grave to prevent him returning. I am glad, and rejoice to see the fellowship of the church delivered from such a contagion; but I am sad and sorry as I reflect that the wretched man never rested from his misdeeds, but died designing greater and worse.

—Theodoret of Cyrrhus (393–457), on the death of his theological adversary, Archbishop Cyril of Alexandria (c. 376–444)

A NEW WORLD

But upon a day the good providence of God did cast me to Bedford to work on my calling, and in one of the streets of that town I came where there were three or four poor women sitting at a door in the sun and talking about the things of God; and being now willing to hear them discourse I drew near to hear what they said, for I was now a brisk talker also myself in the matters of religion. But now I may say I heard, but I understood not; for they were far above, out of my reach; for their talk was about a new birth—the work of God on their hearts. And methought they spake as if joy did make them speak; they spake with such pleasantness of scripture language and with such appearance of grace in all they said, that they were to me as if they had found a new world.

—John Bunyan (1628-1688),
author of The Pilgrim's Progress

THE SEVEN PENITENTIAL PSALMS

Psalms of confession and penitence, often used on Ash Wednesday or during the season of Lent. They number seven:

Psalm 6: "O Lord, rebuke me not in thine anger."
Psalm 32: "Blessed is he whose transgression is forgiven."
Psalm 38: "O Lord, rebuke me not in thy wrath."
Psalm 51: "Have mercy upon me, O God, according to thy lovingkindness."
Psalm 102: "Hear my prayer, O Lord, and let my cry come unto thee."
Psalm 130: "Out of the depths have I cried unto thee, O Lord."
Psalm 143: "Hear my prayer, O Lord, give ear to my supplications."

MORE CORNY CHURCH ADS

Meet the author of the world's best-selling book here.

Life: always read the maker's instructions.
Read the Bible.

Carpenter of Nazareth seeks joiners.

Feeling a bit down in the mouth?
Come in for a faith lift!

2,000 years ago Wise Men searched for Jesus.
Wise people still do!

How are you going to spend eternity—smoking or non-smoking?

God knows when you were last in church.

The best vitamin for a Christian is B1.

God answers knee-mail.

A family altar alters a family.

This church is prayer-conditioned.

Free trip to Heaven!
Details inside.

TGIF—Thank God I'm Forgiven

My life was going to waste—
then Jesus recycled me.

YOU CALL ME . . .

You call me master but obey me not;
You call me light but seek me not;
You call me the way but walk me not;
You call me wise but follow me not;
You call me fair but love me not;
You call me rich but ask me not;

You call me eternal but seek me not;
You call me gracious but trust me not;
You call me noble but serve me not;
You call me mighty but honor me not;
You call me just but fear me not;
If I condemn you, blame me not.

> —*adapted translation of an anonymous inscription in Lübeck Cathedral, Germany. The German original begins: "Ihr nennt mich Meister, so fraget mich doch. / Ihr nennt mich Licht, so seht mich doch."*

THE LOVE CHAPTER

A favorite for weddings. Yet the author, the apostle Paul, was actually arguing that love is more important and lasting than impressive spiritual gifts such as speaking in tongues, asceticism, and prophesying. The King James Version translates the Greek *agapē*—"love"—as "charity," defined by C. S. Lewis as love selflessly committed to the well-being of another.

> [1]Though I speak with the tongues of men and of angels, and have not charity, I am become as sounding brass, or a tinkling cymbal. [2]And though I have the gift of prophecy, and understand all mysteries, and all knowledge; and though I have all faith, so that I could remove mountains, and have not charity, I am nothing. [3]And though I bestow all my goods to feed the poor, and though I give my body to be burned, and have not charity, it profiteth me nothing. [4]Charity suffereth long, and is kind; charity envieth not; charity vaunteth not itself, is not puffed up. [5]Doth not behave itself unseemly, seeketh not her own, is not easily provoked, thinketh no evil; [6]rejoiceth not in iniquity, but rejoiceth in the truth; [7]beareth all things, believeth all things, hopeth all things, endureth all things. [8]Charity never faileth: but whether there be prophecies, they shall fail; whether there be tongues, they shall cease; whether there be knowledge, it shall vanish away. [9]For

we know in part, and we prophesy in part. ¹⁰But when that which is perfect is come, then that which is in part shall be done away. ¹¹When I was a child, I spake as a child, I understood as a child, I thought as a child: but when I became a man, I put away childish things. ¹²For now we see through a glass, darkly; but then face to face: now I know in part; but then shall I know even as also I am known. ¹³And now abideth faith, hope, charity, these three; but the greatest of these is charity.

—*1 Corinthians 13*

HOPE

Your frequently repeated Wishes and Prayers for my Eternal as well as temporal Happiness are very obliging. I have myself no Doubts that I shall enjoy as much of both as is proper for me. That Being who gave me Existence, and thro' almost three score years has been continually showering his Favors upon me, whose very Chastisements have been Blessings to me, can I doubt that he loves me? And if he loves me, can I doubt that he will go on to take care of me not only here but hereafter? This to some may seem Presumption; to me it appears the best grounded Hope; Hope of the Future; built on Experience of the Past.

—*Benjamin Franklin (1706–1790) to the English evangelist George Whitefield, June 19, 1764*

AS THE BISHOP SAID TO THE ACTRESS

A young couple were discussing their wedding with the pastor.
They asked, "Pastor, do you believe in sex before the wedding?"
"Not if it delays the ceremony," he replied.

A novice entered a very strict Order, in which the monks were permitted to speak one sentence to the abbot every five years.

After the first five years the novice went to the abbot and said, "I'm cold."

After another five years the novice went to the abbot and said, "I'm hungry."

After five more years the novice said, "I need a new habit."

"I'm afraid you're not suited to the monastic life," said the abbot. "You've done nothing but complain ever since you got here!"

A Jewish boy attended a service in a Catholic church. Afterward, he described it to his rabbi.

"They said a Jewish prayer!" said the boy excitedly.

"A Jewish prayer?" asked the rabbi. "What was that, then?"

"Oy vey Maria . . ."

WHO WERE THE TWELVE APOSTLES?

This is not the simple question it appears. Although the core group—Andrew, Peter, James, John, etc.—is incontestable, some apostles are given different names in different Gospels and others—for instance, Thaddaeus and Nathanael—are little mentioned. (Lists of apostles can be found in Matthew 10:2-4, Mark 3:16-19, Luke 6:14-16, and Acts 1:13.)

1. Simon Peter, "bar Jonah" (Matt. 16:17), Andrew's brother
2. Andrew (Matt. 4:18), Peter's brother
3. James "the Elder," son of Zebedee, brother of John (Matt. 4:21)
4. John, son of Zebedee, brother of James (Matt. 4:21)
5. Philip (Mark 3:18)
6. Bartholomew (Matt. 10:3), probably identical with Nathanael (John 1:45)
7. Thomas, "the twin" (John 20:24)
8. Matthew, a.k.a. Levi the tax collector (Matt. 10:3; Mark 2:14)
9. James "the Younger" or "the Less," son of Alphaeus (Matt. 10:3)
10. Judas/Jude "the Zealot," a.k.a. Thaddaeus or Lebbaeus (Luke 6:16; "not Iscariot," John 14:22); son or brother of James

11. Simon the Zealot, or Canaanean (Matt. 10:4; Luke 6:15)
12. Judas Iscariot, that is, from Kerioth (Matt. 10:4). After Judas betrayed Christ, the remaining disciples chose Matthias to replace him (Acts 1:26).
13. Saul, a.k.a. Paul, Apostle to the Gentiles (Rom. 11:13), chosen by Jesus (Acts 9:3-6)

PRAYER OF ST. IGNATIUS

Teach us, good Lord,
to serve thee as thou deservest;
to give and not to count the cost;
to fight and not to heed the wounds;
to toil and not to seek for rest;
to labor and not to ask for any reward
save that of knowing that we do thy will.

*—attributed to Ignatius Loyola (1491–1556),
founder of the Society of Jesus*

SOME NATIONAL SAINTS AND THEIR FEAST DAYS

Country	Saint	Feast Day
Algeria	St. Cyprian of Carthage	September 16
Argentina	St. Francis Solano	July 14
Armenia	St. Gregory the Illuminator	September 30
Australia	St. Francis Xavier	December 3
Austria	St. Florian	May 4
Belgium	St. Columbanus of Ghent	February 2
Brazil	St. Antony of Padua	June 13
Bulgaria	St. Cyril the Philosopher	February 14

Cyprus	St. Barnabas	June 11
Denmark	St. Canute	January 19
Egypt	St. Mark the Evangelist	January 17
England	St. George	April 23
Ethiopia	St. Frumentius	October 27
France	St. Joan of Arc	May 30
Germany	St. Boniface	June 5
Gibraltar	St. Bernard of Clairvaux	August 20
Greece	St. Andrew	November 30
Guatemala	St. James the Greater	July 25
Iceland	St. Thorlac Thorhallsson	December 23
India	St. Thomas	July 3
Iran	St. Maruthas of Martyropolis	December 4
Ireland	St. Patrick	March 17
Jordan	St. John the Baptist	June 24
Madagascar	St. Vincent de Paul	September 27
Malta	St. Paul	January 25
Netherlands	St. Bavo	October 1
Norway	St. Olaf II	July 29
Philippines	St. Rose of Lima	August 23
Poland	St. Casimir	March 4
Russia	St. Nicholas	December 6
Scotland	St. Andrew	November 30
Sri Lanka	St. Lawrence	August 10
Sweden	St. Bridget	July 23
Switzerland	St. Gall	October 16
Syria	St. Barbara	December 4
Wales	St. David	March 1

HOLY MOSES . . .

Hollywood actors who have played him include the following:

Mel Brooks in *History of the World, Part I* (1981)
Charlton Heston in *The Ten Commandments* (1956)
Ben Kingsley in *Moses* (1996 TV miniseries)
Burt Lancaster in *Moses, the Lawgiver* (1974)
Dudley Moore in *Wholly Moses!* (1980)
Theodore Roberts in *The Ten Commandments* (1923)
Soupy Sales in *. . . And God Spoke* (1993)
Christian Bale in *Exodus: Gods and Kings* (2014)

WHY IS IT CALLED "THE MASS"?

In the medieval Roman Catholic Church, once the Eucharist was finished, a deacon announced, *"Ite missa est"*—"Go, it's finished."

When the congregation—who didn't understand Latin—heard these words, they knew the service was over. In time, the word *missa* came to stand for the entire service.

In popular Latin, *"missa"* became *"messa"* and passed into Middle English as "masse" or "mass."

FROM "A BETTER RESURRECTION"

> I have no wit, no words, no tears;
> My heart within me like a stone
> Is numb'd too much for hopes or fears;
> Look right, look left, I dwell alone;
> I lift mine eyes, but dimm'd with grief
> No everlasting hills I see;
> My life is in the falling leaf:
> O Jesus, quicken me.
>
> —*Christina Rossetti (1830–1894), English poet*

DENOMINATIONS WITH MEMORABLE NAMES

Church of God with Signs Following: Pentecostal Holiness church that practices snake handling and drinking poison during services to show their members' strong faith.

Two-Seed-in-the-Spirit Predestinarian Baptists: founded by Elder Daniel Parker (1781–1844) in Illinois, 1833.

Assemblies of the Called Out Ones of Yah: founded in 1974 by Sam Surratt, who believed the Creator's name is "Yah" and his son, the Messiah, is "Yeshuah."

No-Name Church (or *Two by Twos*): one of many names used for an international home-based movement founded by William Irvine in Ireland in 1897. Other names include: The Truth, The Black Stockings, Workers and Friends, Cooneyites, and Christians Anonymous.

The Peculiar People: founded by James Banyard in Rochford, Essex, England, in 1838 as an offshoot of the Wesleyan denomination. They derive their name from Deuteronomy 14:2 and 1 Peter 2:9, the latter reading in the King James Version: "But ye are a chosen generation, a royal priesthood, an holy nation, a peculiar people . . ."

I AM

Jesus makes seven statements beginning "I am . . ." in John's Gospel.

1. I am the bread of life (6:35).
2. I am the light of the world (8:12).
3. I am the door (10:9).
4. I am the good shepherd (10:11).
5. I am the resurrection, and the life (11:25).
6. I am the way, the truth, and the life (14:6).
7. I am the true vine (15:1).

WAS THERE A BETHLEHEM STABLE?

There is no mention of a stable in the biblical accounts of Jesus's birth.

Luke's Gospel says there was no room in the inn, and that Mary laid Jesus in a manger—which has led people to assume there must have been a stable.

The Church of the Nativity in Bethlehem is built over a cave or grotto, where tradition has it that Jesus was born. Some early Christian writers also refer to a cave.

Neither does Luke's Gospel mention any animals in the stable: the ox and ass of carols and Christmas cards probably derive from the Old Testament: "The ox knoweth his owner, and the ass his master's crib" (Isa. 1:3).

HOW TO SPEAK OF GOD

Jews believe the name of the Almighty is too holy to be voiced. They use a number of terms to avoid enunciating the word "God," including:

Adonai ("my Lord")
Elohim ("God")
YHWH (Yahweh)
King of Kings
Hashem ("the name")
Master of the Universe
El Elyon ("Most High God")
Shaddai ("Almighty")
Ha-Kadosh Baruch Hu ("Holy One Blessed Be He")
G-D

"TERESA'S BOOKMARK"

Let nothing disturb thee,
Nothing affright thee;
All things are passing;
God never changeth.
Patient endurance
Attaineth to all things;
Who God possesseth
In nothing is wanting;
Alone God sufficeth.

*—Teresa of Ávila (1515–1582), Spanish mystic,
translated by Henry Wadsworth Longfellow*

THE FOUR HORSEMEN OF THE APOCALYPSE

The much-cited horsemen of Revelation 6:1–8, feared as harbingers of doom.

First horseman: Pestilence
On a white horse, with a bow, "went forth conquering, and to conquer."

Second horseman: War
On a red horse, with a large sword, had power to take peace from the earth.

Third horseman: Famine
On a black horse. He holds a pair of scales and is traditionally named famine.

Fourth horseman: Death
On a pale horse. Death and hell are given power "to kill with sword, and with hunger, and with death, and with the beasts of the earth."

ICHTHUS

An *ichthus* is an ancient Christian rebus code that is spelled out as follows:

i-ch-th-u-s = ***I****esous **Ch**ristos **Th**eou **U**ios **S**oter*
(Jesus Christ, God's Son, Savior)

The Greek word for fish, *ichthus*, has been used since the first century to symbolize the Savior, Jesus Christ. The fish symbol was a rebus by which early Christians identified each other, particularly in times of persecution. When scrawled on a wall or on the ground, it told Christians that others of their faith were nearby.

VARIETIES OF MONKS

Cenobites	Monks belonging to a monastic community
Cloistered	Monks who never leave their building or compound
Discalced	Monks who wear no shoes. Today, they wear sandals!
Hermits	Monks who withdraw to a solitary life, often in a cave, sometimes in a loose community with others
Anchorites	Monks who withdraw to a solitary ascetic life of silence and prayer, sometimes in a walled-up cell
Stylites	Simeon Stylites (390–459) lived near Antioch atop a pillar whose height was increased gradually to sixty feet. Other "stylites" followed his example.

BEREAVEMENT

They that love beyond the world cannot be separated by it. Death cannot kill what never dies. Nor can spirits ever be divided that love and live in the same divine principle, the root and record of their friendship. If absence be not death, neither is theirs.

> Death is but crossing the world, as friends do the seas; they live in one another still. For they must needs be present, that love and live in that which is omnipresent. . . .
>
> This is the comfort of friends, that though they may be said to die, yet their friendship and society are ever present, in the best sense, because immortal.
>
> —William Penn (1644-1718), *early member of the Religious Society of Friends (Quakers)*

THE TRIBES OF ISRAEL

They are named for the sons of Jacob and include the following:

1. Reuben (mother, Leah)
2. Simeon (Leah)
3. Levi (Leah), the priestly tribe, allotted no territory
4. Judah (Leah)
5. Dan (mother, Bilhah)
6. Naphtali (Bilhah)
7. Gad (mother, Zilpah)
8. Asher (Zilpah)
9. Issachar (Leah)
10. Zebulun (Leah)
11. Ephraim (son of Joseph)
12. Manasseh (son of Joseph)
13. Benjamin (mother, Rachel)

Why thirteen tribes when we normally speak of the "twelve tribes of Israel"? Unlike the other tribes, Levi didn't receive territory. Also, Joseph's sons were considered heads of their own tribes— both of which received an inheritance of land. In some Old Testament lists, Joseph is counted as one of the twelve. In others, Levi isn't counted and Ephraim and Manasseh are named as separate tribes. Confusing!

MORE PECULIAR PARSONS

Rev. John Keate, headmaster of Eton College, after a pupil rebellion in 1832, flogged eighty boys in a day.

Rev. Charles Tennyson, nineteenth-century curate of Tealby, Lincolnshire, became addicted to opium and dressed in rabbit skins.

Rev. Henry Prince declared himself Messiah on New Year's Day 1846, withdrawing with his followers to a house in Somerset to form the Church of the Agapemone, or "Abode of Love."

In 1879 Rev. John Thorneycroft Hartley, a vicar in north Yorkshire, reached the men's singles tennis semifinals at Wimbledon. After the quarterfinal on Saturday, he traveled 250 miles to Yorkshire to conduct Sunday services, returning for the semifinal on Monday morning—but lost 6-0, 6-0, 6-0.

In 1925 Westminster Abbey objected to broadcasting the wedding of the Duke of York (later King George VI), fearing that it "might even be received by persons in public houses with their hats on."

Rev. Harold Davidson, rector of Stiffkey (normally pronounced Stewkey), Norfolk, was defrocked for immoral practices with young women in London's West End. He died in 1937, after being savaged while speaking to seaside holidaymakers from a lion's cage.

Lord Rupert Ernest William Gascoyne-Cecil, bishop of Exeter, 1916-1936, had a reputation for eccentricity. He fed crumpets to rats, complained that the Bible was an "awkward book," and often rang his wife to discover where he was when traveling around his diocese.

STATIONS OF THE CROSS (*VIA CRUCIS* OR *VIA DOLOROSA*)

This fourteen-stage Catholic processional devotion follows Jesus's last journey from his trial to his burial, with depictions of each scene placed around the church building.

First Station
Jesus is condemned to death.

Second Station
Jesus accepts and carries his cross.

Third Station
Jesus falls for the first time.

Fourth Station
Jesus meets his mother, Mary.

Fifth Station
Simon of Cyrene helps Jesus carry his cross.

Sixth Station
Veronica wipes Jesus's face.

Seventh Station
Jesus falls a second time.

Eighth Station
Jesus meets women of Jerusalem and asks them not to weep for him.

Ninth Station
Jesus falls a third time.

Tenth Station
Jesus is stripped, and his clothes are taken by Roman soldiers.

Eleventh Station
Jesus is nailed to the cross.

Twelfth Station
Jesus dies on the cross.

Thirteenth Station
Jesus's body is taken down from the cross.

Fourteenth Station
Jesus's body is laid in the tomb.

"LOVE"

Love bade me welcome: yet my soul drew back,
    Guilty of dust and sin.
But quick-ey'd Love, observing me grow slack
    From my first entrance in,
Drew nearer to me, sweetly questioning,
    If I lack'd any thing.

A guest, I answer'd, worthy to be here:
    Love said, You shall be he.
I the unkind, ungrateful? Ah my dear,
    I cannot look on thee.
Love took my hand, and smiling did reply,
    Who made the eyes but I?

Truth Lord, but I have marr'd them: let my shame
    Go where it doth deserve.
And know you not, says Love, who bore the blame?
    My dear, then I will serve.
You must sit down, says Love, and taste my meat:
    So I did sit and eat.

—George Herbert (1593–1633), priest and poet

TITLES FOR THE BIBLE

The Holy Bible
The Book
The Good Book
The Book of Books
Scripture
The Scriptures

Holy Writ
The Word
The Word of God

THE SEPTUAGINT AND VULGATE

The Septuagint is the Greek translation of the Hebrew Bible (the Christian "Old Testament"), made in Egypt in the third and second centuries BCE.

The word "Septuagint," often abbreviated LXX (Roman numerals for seventy), is derived from the Latin *septuaginta*, "seventy."

According to legend, seventy-two translators, six from each of the twelve tribes of Israel, separately translated the entire Bible—and all seventy-two versions emerged identical. The Septuagint was the version of the Old Testament used by most early Christian communities. It includes several books not found in the Hebrew Bible, such as additions to the book of Esther.

And the Vulgate?

The Vulgate is the Latin translation of the Bible made by St. Jerome, completed in 405 CE.

The word "Vulgate" is derived from the Latin "*vulgata editio*," meaning "edition for common use." In 1546, the reforming Roman Catholic Council of Trent decreed the Vulgate to be the sole authoritative Latin version of the Bible.

THE SEVEN DEADLY SINS AND
THE SEVEN VIRTUES

The "Seven Deadly Sins" are derived from a list drawn up by the fourth-century monk Evagrius Ponticus.

He listed eight evils in Greek:	**They are translated into Latin as:**
Γαστριμαργία (*gastrimargia*)	*Gula* (gluttony)
Πορνεία (*porneia*)	*Fornicatio* (fornication, lust)

Greek:	Latin:
Φιλαργυρία (*philargyria*)	*Avaritia* (avarice, greed)
Λύπη (*lypē*)	*Tristitia* (sorrow, despair)
Ὀργή (*orgē*)	*Ira* (wrath, anger)
Ἀκηδία (*akēdia*)	*Acedia* (sloth)
Κενοδοξία (*kenodoxia*)	*Vanagloria* (vainglory)
Ὑπερηφανία (*hyperēphania*)	*Superbia* (pride)

Of these, despair is omitted from the modern listing.

The seven virtues, as adopted by the early church fathers:

1. Chastity
2. Temperance
3. Charity
4. Diligence
5. Patience
6. Kindness
7. Humility

THE TETRAGRAMMATON

"Yahweh" is the only *name* of God in the Bible; all other terms are titles.

The name "Yahweh" is linked to a Hebrew verb for "to be," and can mean "I am" or "he who is."

Hebrew words were written with consonants alone, and "Yahweh" may be written YHWH—often referred to as the *Tetragrammaton*—"the word of four letters," from the Greek *tetra*, "four," and *gramma*, "letter."

Because the Jews believed the name "Yahweh" too holy to pronounce, they used *Adonai* ("my Lord") instead when the Hebrew Bible was read aloud. In many Bible versions, "Yahweh" is translated as "the Lord."

Over time, the vowels of the word *Adonai* were combined with the consonants in YHWH to create the word *Iehouah* in medieval Latin—"Jehovah" in modern English.

JACOB'S PILLOW

According to tradition, the stone that Jacob used as a pillow in the wilderness (Gen. 28:11), when fleeing his furious brother Esau, was later taken to Egypt by his sons. From there it was supposedly carried to Spain, and thence to Ireland, where it became the stone on which Irish kings sat to be crowned and became known as the "fatal stone" or "stone of destiny."

From Ireland it was taken to Scotland, serving as the stone upon which Scots kings were crowned until the end of the thirteenth century. After defeating the Scots, King Edward I of England moved the stone to Westminster Abbey in 1296, where it became part of the Coronation Chair. Alternatively known as the "Stone of Scone," it was returned to Scotland in 1996.

THE SEVEN SORROWS OF THE VIRGIN MARY

This is a traditional Catholic list of events that brought sorrow to Jesus's mother.

1. Simeon's prophecy that "a sword shall pierce through thy own soul also" (Luke 2:34–35)
2. The flight of the holy family into Egypt to escape Herod (Matt. 2:13–14)
3. Losing youthful Jesus in the temple when returning from Jerusalem (Luke 2:42–45)
4. Meeting Jesus on his way to the cross (Luke 23:27–28)
5. Standing at the foot of the cross (John 19:26)
6. Watching Jesus taken down from the cross (Luke 23:53)
7. Jesus's entombment (John 19:41–42)

WHO WROTE THE KING JAMES VERSION?

Not King James I—he merely "authorized" it.

The King James Version (KJV) is the most-read work of English literature, an example of the English language at its most eloquent, subtle, and beautiful, published in 1611, when Shakespeare's great tragedies were first being performed at London's Globe theater.

The King James Version was created by a team. The text was the work of six committees, two from Oxford University (Isaiah through Malachi, the Gospels, Acts, and Revelation), two from Cambridge (Chronicles through Ecclesiastes and the Apocrypha), and two from Westminster (Genesis through Kings and Romans through Jude), drawing overall on the expertise of fifty scholars.

The translation was next checked and revised by twelve of the team, with Archbishop Richard Bancroft acting as "chief overseer."

The Oxford translators included Dr. Richard Brett, who was "skilled and versed to a criticism in the Latin, Greek, Hebrew, Chaldee, Arabic, and Ethiopic tongues," and Dr. Miles Smith, who "had Hebrew at his fingers' ends." The Cambridge group boasted Dr. Lawrence Chadderton, who was "familiar with the Greek and Hebrew tongues, and the numerous writings of the Rabbis," and John Bois, "a precious Greek and Hebrew scholar." Meanwhile, at Westminster there was Lancelot Andrewes, "who might have been interpreter general at Babel."

The translators' brief was to follow, as far as possible, the 1602 edition of the Bishops' Bible, first published in 1586. However, it has been estimated that roughly 80 percent of the King James Version is derived from William Tyndale's pioneering English translation, produced in the reign of Henry VIII, and around 19 percent from the Geneva Bible of 1560.

So who made the KJV? William Tyndale, with quite a lot of help.

TEN TERRIFYING EXORCISM MOVIES

The Exorcist (1973)   *The Last Exorcism* (2010)

The Exorcist III (1990)   *The Rite* (2011)

Beloved (1998)	*The Conjuring* (2013)
Stigmata (1999)	*Deliver Us from Evil* (2014)
The Exorcism of Emily Rose (2005)	*The Conjuring 2* (2016)

DOES THE BIBLE REALLY SAY THAT?

Adam's apple?

According to the book of Genesis, Adam and Eve didn't eat an apple. The fruit they tasted is simply referred to as the fruit of the "tree of the knowledge of good and evil" (Gen. 2:17).

So, why an apple? In Middle English, "apple" referred to all fruit and nuts apart from berries, leading to the Hebrew word for "fruit" being translated "apple."

The projection formed by the larynx at the front of the human throat is known as the "Adam's apple"; legend has it that a piece of the forbidden fruit got stuck in our first father's throat.

That serpent, Satan?

In the story of the fall in Genesis, the serpent that persuaded Eve to take the fruit from the tree is simply described as "more subtil than any beast of the field"—but never named as "Satan."

Jonah and the whale?

The book of Jonah says God sent "a great fish"—not a whale—to swallow the prophet Jonah when he was thrown overboard in a storm.

Mary Magdalene a prostitute?

The Bible never describes Mary Magdalene (Mary of Magdala) as a prostitute. In fact, she is scarcely mentioned. Apart from her presence at the resurrection (Luke 24:10), the only other reference to her is Jesus's curing her of seven demons (Luke 8:2).

The prodigal son—a runaway?

The word "prodigal" doesn't occur in the Bible story about the runaway son. It was added as a subheading and means "wasteful" or "lavish," presumably referring to his lifestyle in exile: it has nothing to do with leaving home—or indeed returning (Luke 15:11–32).

HOW MANY CRUSADES?

In 1071 Seljuk Turks captured Jerusalem and conquered most of Asia Minor, seriously weakening the Eastern Roman Empire. Responding to an appeal from Emperor Alexius I Comnenus, Pope Urban II (r. 1088–1099) appealed for an expedition to recover the Holy Land. The series of crusades followed.

First Crusade (1096–1099)	Captured Antioch and established the Latin Kingdom of Jerusalem.
Second Crusade (1147–1149)	Most Crusaders never reached the Holy Land.
Third Crusade (1188–1192)	The Syrian ruler Saladin recaptured Jerusalem in 1187. Richard I of England, "The Lionheart," agreed to a truce that allowed Crusaders to visit Jerusalem.
Fourth Crusade (1202–1204)	Installed a Western ruler on the throne of the Eastern Empire in Constantinople—but never reached the Holy Land.
Children's Crusade (1212)	Few children reached even the ports of France and Italy to embark for the Holy Land.
Fifth Crusade (1217–1221)	Mainly took place in Egypt—but recovered the "true cross."
Sixth Crusade (1228–1229)	Frederick II, Holy Roman emperor, governed Jerusalem for fifteen years, until its final recapture by the Turks in 1244.
Seventh Crusade (1248–1254)	Louis IX of France strengthened Christian enclaves in Syria but failed to retake Jerusalem.
Eighth Crusade (1270)	Louis IX died in Tunis; Christian footholds remaining in Syria were lost.

SOME TITLES FOR JESUS

Bread of Life	Messiah
Dayspring	Our Lord
First and Last	Our Passover
Good Shepherd	Prince of Peace
Holy One of God	Redeemer
Horn of Salvation	Savior
Immanuel	Son of David
King of Kings	Son of God
King of the Jews	Son of Man
Lamb of God	Son of the Highest
Last Adam	The Amen
Light of the World	The Word
Man of Sorrows	True Vine

STIGMATICS

Stigmata are marks, sores, or painful sensations located in similar places on the body to the wounds of the crucified Christ, usually appearing during religious ecstasy or hysteria. People bearing the stigmata—"stigmatics"—are not heard of before the thirteenth century. The Catholic Church officially recognizes sixty-two stigmatics.

Among the best known are:

St. Francis of Assisi (1186–1226)—the first reported to have received the stigmata
St. Margaret of Cortona (1247–1297)
St. Gertrude (1256–1302)
St. Clare of Montefalco (1268–1308)
St. Catherine of Siena (1347–1380)
St. Rita of Cassia (1386–1456)
St. Catherine of Genoa (1447–1510)

Lucy of Narni (1476–1547)—one of two Lucys after whom C. S. Lewis named Lucy Pevensie in his Narnia Chronicles. Narnia was named for Narni, a small town in Umbria, Italy.

St. John of God (1495–1550)

St. Mary Magdalene de' Pazzi (1566–1607)

St. Veronica Giuliani (1660–1727)

St. Mary Frances of the Five Wounds (1715–1791)

St. Pio of Pietrelcina ("Padre Pio") (1887–1968)

MILLENNIALISMS

Christians have many differing views about the millennium. The word "millennium" derives from Latin for "one thousand years," a period mentioned in Revelation 20. Millennial views vary according to how Christ's return—second coming or second advent—is related to this thousand-year period.

Premillennialism

In this version, Christ returns to inaugurate his kingdom before the millennium.

Most premillennialists expect a seven-year period of "tribulation"—cataclysmic events—preceding his appearance. There are subcategories of premillennialism, based on the timing of the "rapture," or "catching up," of Christians, suggested in 1 Thessalonians 4:17:

a. Pretribulationism—the church is raptured before the tribulation
b. Posttribulationalism—the church is raptured after the tribulation
c. Midtribulationism—the church is raptured during the tribulation

Postmillennialism

According to this view, the millennium is a period of righteousness, peace, and blessing brought about by the advance of the gospel and increasing influence of God's kingdom. At the end of the millennium, Christ will return for general resurrection and judgment.

Amillennialism

In this view, the millennium is a symbolic concept describing the present rule of Christ in the church. The "last days" began with Jesus's resurrection and ascension, and the "tribulation" refers to the events of the first century CE that led to the destruction of Jerusalem and Herod's temple. Christ will return for judgment after his present reign, and believers enter the kingdom through new life in Christ now and at their death.

HEAVEN

> When I go to heaven, I shall see three wonders there—the first wonder will be to see any people there whom I did not expect to see; the second wonder will be to miss many people whom I did expect to see; and the third and greatest wonder of all will be to find myself there.
>
> —*John Newton (1725–1807), English hymn writer*

> When you speak of heaven let your features be irradiated with a heavenly light.... But when you talk about hell—your ordinary face will do.
>
> —*Charles Haddon Spurgeon (1834–1892),*
> *English Baptist, instructing young ministers*

> We may be surprised at the people we find in heaven. God has a soft spot for sinners.
>
> —*Desmond Tutu (1931–), South African theologian*

> My home is in heaven. I'm just traveling through this world.
>
> —*Billy Graham (1918–2018), American evangelist*

CLERGY DRESS

Clerical attire is often a good indicator of the type of church a priest serves: the more traditional the garb, the more traditional the church. The technical term for clerical gear is "vestments."

Here are a few:

Chasuble: seamless outer cloak worn during Eucharist
Maniple: strip worn over the left wrist during Eucharist, representing the cloth Jesus might have used to wash his disciples' feet
Pallium: strip of white wool with six embedded crosses worn across the shoulders
Stole: long scarf symbolizing humility, worn around the neck or over one arm during Eucharist
Alb: All-in-one tunic symbolizing purity
Cassock: priest's black dress

HUMILITY

> If you should ask me the ways of God, I would tell you the first is humility, the second is humility, and the third is still humility.
>
> —*Augustine of Hippo (354–430), North African theologian*

> I used to think that God's gifts were on shelves one above the other and that the taller we grew in Christian character the more easily we could reach them. I now find that God's gifts are on shelves one beneath the other and that it is not a question of growing taller but of stooping lower.
>
> —*F. B. Meyer (1847–1929), Baptist pastor*

Humility is not thinking less of yourself, it's thinking of yourself less.

—C. S. Lewis (1898-1963), English writer

SEVEN SACRAMENTS

The Roman Catholic and Orthodox Churches recognize seven sacraments—important and significant rites. Protestant churches recognize fewer, and often call them "ordinances" rather than sacraments.

1. Eucharist—also known as Holy Communion or the Lord's Supper
2. Baptism
3. Confirmation—Chrismation in the Orthodox Church
4. Confession—also known as Penance and Reconciliation
5. Matrimony, or Marriage
6. Holy Orders, or Ordination
7. Extreme Unction—Anointing of the Sick

MORE BIBLE MISPRINTS

Sin On Bible (KJV, 1716)
Perhaps the most infamous misprinted Bible. John 5:14—"sin no more"—appears as "sin on more."

Vinegar Bible (KJV, Oxford, 1717)
The heading for Luke chapter 20 reads "Parable of the Vinegar" rather than "Vineyard."

Fool Bible (KJV, 1763)
Reads "The fool hath said in his heart there is a God," instead of "there is no God" (Ps. 14:1). The printer was fined £3,000 (a huge sum for the period) and all copies were ordered destroyed.

Child-Killer Bible (KJV, 1795)
Mark 7:27 reads, "Let the children first be killed," rather than "filled."

To Remain Bible (KJV, 1805)
Galatians 4:29—"persecuted him that was born after the Spirit, even so it is now"—appeared as "persecuted him that was born after the spirit to remain, even so it is now." The words "to remain" were a note from the editor that the comma after the word "spirit" should not be deleted. The printer thought it meant he should add the words "to remain."

Pay for Peace Bible (Jerusalem Bible, 1966)
Psalm 122:6 reads "pay for peace" rather than "pray for peace."

Rebekah's Camels Bible (KJV, 1823)
Genesis 24:61 reads "Rebekah arose, and her camels" instead of "damsels."

UNNAMED

Apocryphal texts and tradition have bestowed names on some Bible characters who are otherwise nameless.

Awan	Cain's wife (book of Jubilees)
Emzara	Noah's wife (book of Jubilees)
Ne'elatama'uk, Sedeqetelebab, Adataneses	Wives of Noah's sons: Ham, Shem, and Japheth
Edna	Abraham's mother (book of Jubilees)
Zuleika	Potiphar's wife, who attempted to seduce Joseph
Bithiah or Thebatis	Pharaoh's daughter, who adopted Moses after rescuing him from the Nile River
Sitis (or Sitidos) and Dinah	Job's wives

Caspar, Melchior, Balthasar, or Larvandad, Hormisdad, and Gushnasaph	The wise men, or Magi, who visited the infant Jesus
Phineas, Neves, Amonofis, or Tantalus	The rich man (Dives) who ignored the beggar Lazarus
Bernice or Josephia	Woman Jesus healed of bleeding (Matt. 9)
Procla/Procula, Claudia, or Perpetua	Pilate's wife, who dreamt about Jesus's trial
Dismas/Dysmas	The "good thief" crucified next to Jesus
Gestas	The unrepentant thief, crucified beside Jesus

WHAT A WAY TO GO

Some Bible characters who died in unpleasant ways:

Nadab and Abihu: consumed by fire (Lev. 10:1–2)
Korah, his family, and all his men: swallowed up by the earth (Num. 16:1–35)
Amorites: killed by huge hailstones (Josh. 10:8–14)
Absalom: suspended by his own hair (2 Sam. 18:9)
Abimelech: killed by a millstone thrown from a city wall (2 Sam. 11:21)
Sisera: killed by a tent peg hammered through his temple by Jael (Judg. 4:18–21)
Haman: hanged on gallows he had constructed to hang another man (Esther 7:10–8:2)
Herod Agrippa: eaten by worms (Acts 12:23)

FIVE POINTS OF CALVINISM

These are doctrines claiming to summarize the results of the Synod of Dort (1618–1619) in the Netherlands, set up to resolve a dispute about Arminian theology within the Calvinist Dutch Reformed church. Remembered by the mnemonic "TULIP":

Total Depravity—through the fall, every aspect of humanity is stained by sin: we cannot save ourselves.
Unconditional Election (predestination)—God chooses who will be saved and who will be damned.
Limited Atonement—Christ died for the sins of the elect alone.
Irresistible Grace—the elect are powerless to resist God's salvation.
Perseverance of the Saints—the elect cannot lose their salvation.

Jefferson's response:

> I can never join Calvin in addressing his god. He was indeed an Atheist, which I can never be; or rather his religion was Daemonism. If ever man worshipped a false god, he did. The being described in his 5 points is not the God whom you and I acknolege [sic] and adore, the Creator and benevolent governor of the world; but a daemon of malignant spirit. It would be more pardonable to believe in no god at all, than to blaspheme him by the atrocious attributes of Calvin.
>
> —*Thomas Jefferson to John Adams, April 11, 1823*

CONTENTMENT

He that is down needs fear no fall;
He that is low, no pride;
He that is humble ever shall
Have God to be his guide.

I am content with what I have,
Little be it or much:
And, Lord, contentment still I crave,
Because thou savest such.

—*John Bunyan (1628–1688)*

SOME SCRIPTURAL TITLES FOR THE HOLY SPIRIT

The Comforter
The Holy Ghost
The Paraclete
The Spirit of Christ
The Spirit of God
The Spirit of Life
The Spirit of the Lord
The Spirit of Truth
The Spirit of Wisdom and Understanding

ADAM'S FIRST WIFE

According to a nonbiblical myth, Adam's first wife was not Eve but Lilith, who was banished from the garden of Eden because she would not submit to Adam's authority.

Only then did God create Eve.

According to this myth, Lilith subsequently became a demon who stole and killed the newborn.

"REMEMBER"

Remember me when I am gone away,
Gone far away into the silent land;
When you can no more hold me by the hand,
Nor I half turn to go, yet turning stay.
Remember me when no more day by day
You tell me of our future that you plann'd:
Only remember me; you understand
It will be late to counsel then or pray.
Yet if you should forget me for a while
And afterwards remember, do not grieve:
For if the darkness and corruption leave

A vestige of the thoughts that once I had,
Better by far you should forget and smile
Than that you should remember and be sad.

—*Christina Rossetti (1830–1894), English poet*

MR. VALIANT-FOR-TRUTH PASSES OVER

After this it was noised abroad that Mr Valiant-for-truth was taken with a Summons; by the same Post as the other, and had this for a Token that the Summons was true, That his Pitcher was broken at the Fountain. When he understood it, he called for his Friends, and told them of it. Then said he, I am going to my Father's, and though with great Difficulty I am got hither, yet now I do not repent me of all the Trouble I have been at to arrive where I am. My Sword I give to him that shall succeed me in my Pilgrimage, and my Courage and Skill to him that can get it. My Marks and Scars I carry with me, to be a Witness for me, that I have fought his Battles, who now will be my Rewarder. When the Day that he must go hence was come, many accompanied him to the River side, into which as he went he said, Death, where is thy Sting? And as he went down deeper, he said, Grave, where is thy Victory? So he passed over, and all the Trumpets sounded for him on the other side.

—*from* Pilgrim's Progress, *John Bunyan (1628–1688),*
English preacher and writer

THE SEVEN CHURCHES OF REVELATION

St. John the Divine sent a message from Christ to each of these churches in the Roman province of Asia Minor.

1. Ephesus: "I know thy works, and thy labour, and thy patience" (Rev. 2:2)

2. Smyrna: "I know thy works, and tribulation, and poverty" (Rev. 2:9)
3. Pergamum: "I know thy works, and where thou dwellest" (Rev. 2:13)
4. Thyatira: "I know thy works, and charity, and service, and faith" (Rev. 2:19)
5. Sardis: "I know thy works, that thou hast a name that thou livest, and art dead" (Rev. 3:1)
6. Philadelphia: "I know thy works: behold, I have set before thee an open door" (Rev. 3:8)
7. Laodicea: "I know thy works, that thou art neither cold nor hot" (Rev. 3:15)

SEVEN ECUMENICAL COUNCILS

The Catholic and Orthodox churches recognize seven ancient councils of the church, the "Ecumenical Councils."

The councils—and the theological problems they debated:

1. Nicea (325 CE): Arianism
2. Constantinople I (381): Apollinarianism
3. Ephesus (431): Nestorianism
4. Chalcedon (451): Eutychianism
5. Constantinople II (553): Nestorianism and Origenism
6. Constantinople III (680-681): monothelitism
7. Nicea II (787): iconoclasm

Even such abstruse subjects have become the subject of limericks:

> There once was a parson called Arius,
> Whose doctrinal errors were various;
> Of demeanor ascetic
> But opinions heretic,
> The Logos he made secundarius.

A classical man, Apollinarius,
Revived some of the tenets of Arius;
In Laodicea
He had the idea
There could not be two persons contrarious.

—Anonymous

WITCHES AND THE BIBLE

In medieval Europe, a person suspected of witchcraft could be weighed on a huge balance against a heavy Bible. A person who weighed more than the Bible was freed; one lighter than the Bible was deemed guilty of witchcraft.

As late as 1759, this test was forced on an old woman in Aylesbury, Buckinghamshire, England.

BIBLES GREAT AND SMALL

One of the world's largest Bibles is the *Codex Gigas*, measuring 36 × 20 inches (92 × 50.5 cm) and weighing 165 pounds (75 kg). The vellum for its pages is estimated to have required the skin of 160 donkeys. Its 624 pages contain both the Old and New Testaments—plus formulae for treating disease and discovering thieves. Written around 1229, it was stolen from Prague by Swedish soldiers in 1648 during the Thirty Years War.

Legend claims that the *Codex Gigas*, known as the Devil's Bible, was written by one monk in a single night, aided by the devil—although scholars reckon it must have taken up to twenty years to complete. According to the story, the monk was sentenced to be walled up and die a slow death for a dreadful sin but promised freedom if he could create the biggest Bible ever. With just one night to achieve his task, the monk enlisted the devil's aid.

In 1930 Louis Waynai of Los Angeles created a huge copy of the King James Version, using a large homemade rubber-stamp press.

His book runs to 8,048 pages, weighs 1,094 pounds (496 kg), and measures 43.5 inches tall and 98 inches wide (110 × 250 cm), with a spine 34 inches (86 cm) thick.

The "Thumb Bible," printed in 1670, 1 inch square and 1/2 inch thick, had to be read with the aid of a magnifying glass.

Possibly the smallest complete Bible was printed for Glasgow University Press in 1896 by David Bryce & Son of Glasgow and Henry Frowde of London. With pages measuring about 1 ⅝ × 1 ⅛ inches (4 × 2.8 cm), it contains 876 pages and is less than half an inch thick. It was packaged in a case that included a magnifying glass, and 25,000 copies were printed.

Nanotechnology has allowed further miniaturization. A 1,600-page version of the Bible is available on a screen the size of a matchbox. Letters measure 0.0002 inches high, and it is read by means of a 100x magnifier.

A Greek version of the Bible has been printed on a crystal less than 1 inch in diameter.

The world's smallest Hebrew Bible was created at Israel's Technion Institute of Technology in 2007. More than 300,000 words were etched on a gold-coated silicon chip 0.01 inches (0.5 mm) square—smaller than a pinhead.

LANDMARK BIBLE MOVIES

Quo Vadis? (1951)
Based on the legend that, as Peter was fleeing death in Rome, he met Jesus. "*Quo vadis?*" ("Where are you going, Lord?") he asked. Jesus replied, "To Rome, to be crucified again."
Peter turned back to meet his death.
Directed by Mervin LeRoy, with Peter Ustinov as Nero.

The Robe (1953)
At the crucifixion, the centurion Marcellus wins Jesus's robe. Tormented by nightmares, he seeks to find out about the man he has killed. Adapted from Lloyd C. Douglas's best seller

and directed by Henry Koster, with Richard Burton as Marcellus, Jean Simmons as a Roman maid, and Victor Mature as a converted slave.

The Ten Commandments (1956)
Spectacular biblical epic by Cecil B. DeMille telling the story of Moses (Charlton Heston) leading the Israelites out of slavery in Egypt, featuring a celebrated parting of the Red Sea. A remake of DeMille's silent 1923 version, it runs nearly four hours and was called "simultaneously ludicrous and splendid" by a critic.

Ben-Hur (1959)
Adapted from Lew Wallace's novel and directed by William Wyler, with Charlton Heston as Ben-Hur; Stephen Boyd as his nemesis, Messala; and Jack Hawkins as a Roman admiral. The film required more than three hundred sets, and the celebrated twenty-minute chariot race took three months to shoot.

The Gospel according to St. Matthew (1964)
Retold as the story of an ordinary man on a spiritual mission to a rough people in stark surroundings. Directed by Marxist atheist Pier Paolo Pasolini in southern Italy and filmed in black and white with a nonprofessional cast.

The Greatest Story Ever Told (1965)
Four-hour epic about Jesus, directed by George Stevens, with Max von Sydow as Jesus, Telly Savalas as Pilate, Charlton Heston as John the Baptist, David McCallum as Judas, John Wayne as a Roman centurion, and Sidney Poitier as Simon of Cyrene.

The Bible (1966)
John Huston directed, played Noah, and even provided the voice of God. Despite its title, the film only reached halfway through Genesis.

The Life of Brian (1979)
Directed by Terry Jones and written by the Monty Python team, this parody of Hollywood biblical epics recounts the life of Brian of Nazareth, a dumb would-be freedom fighter, whose life parallels Jesus. Though the film is attacked for being anti-Christian, the Pythons' real target is religious zealotry.

The Passion of the Christ (2004)
Directed by Mel Gibson, this film is a brutal, graphic account of the crucifixion, starring Jim Caviezel as Jesus, with subtitles translating the Aramaic and Latin dialogue. Critics accused the film of anti-Semitism.

LEGENDS OF THE SAINTS

St. Apollonia was seized in Alexandria, beaten, and had her teeth knocked out. When her assailants threatened to burn her unless she renounced her faith, she voluntarily jumped into the flames. The patron of dentists, she is typically depicted either holding her tooth with pincers or wearing a necklace housing a gold tooth.

St. Margaret of Antioch, jailed for converting to Christianity, met the devil in the form of a dragon. It swallowed her, but when her cross irritated its belly she emerged intact. Her persecutors failed to kill her by drowning or by fire but succeeded finally in beheading her. Patron of childbirth, she is often depicted emerging, cross in hand, from the dragon's belly.

St. Christopher came from a North African tribe. One legend has him bearing an infant who became increasingly heavy across a river. The child revealed he was Christ, bearing the weight of the world. Christopher is regarded as the protector of travelers.

St. Roch, born into a noble family, traveled widely, healing plague victims. When he himself contracted the plague, a dog licked sores on his leg to heal him. Depicted lifting his hem to display his sores, Roch is patron saint of dogs.

> *St. Denis* was beheaded for his faith. Legend has it that, following decapitation, he picked up his head and walked several miles with it under his arm, preaching as he went. Depicted as a body holding its head in its hands.

SOME CLASSIC HYMNS

For almost every one of the following hymns, it is without question the tune that ensures its continuing popularity.

The title of each hymn is followed by its lyricist, the name of the melody, and, occasionally, its composer.

- "Amazing Grace"—John Newton, England (1779); Amazing Grace/New Britain, trad.
- "How Great Thou Art"—Carl Gustav Boberg, Sweden (1885); *O Store Gud*, trad. Swedish
- "Holy, Holy, Holy"—Reginald Heber, England (1826); Nicaea, John Bacchus Dykes (1861)
- "Great Is Thy Faithfulness"—Thomas Chisholm, Kansas, USA (1923); Faithfulness, William Marion Runyon (1923)
- "When I Survey the Wondrous Cross"—Isaac Watts, England (1707); Rockingham, Edward Miller
- "A Mighty Fortress Is Our God"—Martin Luther, Germany (1527-1529); *Ein Feste Burg*
- "Just As I Am"—Charlotte Elliot (1834); Woodworth, William Bradbury (c. 1849)
- "At the Cross (Alas! And Did My Savior Bleed)"—Isaac Watts, England (1707); Hudson, Ralph Hudson (1885)
- "What a Friend We Have in Jesus"—Joseph M. Scriven (1855); Converse, Charles Converse (1868)
- "All Hail the Power of Jesus' Name"—Edward Perronet (1779); Diadem, James Ellor (1838)
- "Praise to the Lord, the Almighty"—Joachim Neander (1680); *Lobe den Herren*, anonymous
- "Rock of Ages"—Augustus M. Toplady (1776); Toplady, Thomas Hastings (1830)

"Christ the Lord Is Risen Today"—Charles Wesley (1939); Easter Hymn (1708)

"Blessed Assurance"—Fanny Crosby (1873); Assurance, Phoebe Knapp (1873)

"To God Be the Glory"—Fanny Crosby (1872); "To God Be the Glory," William Doane (1875)

"The Old Rugged Cross"—George Bennard (1913); Old Rugged Cross, George Bennard (1913)

"O for a Thousand Tongues to Sing"—Charles Wesley (1739); Lyngham, Thomas Jarman (c. 1803)

"Just a Closer Walk with Thee"—anonymous (date unknown); Closer Walk, trad.

"Turn Your Eyes upon Jesus"—Helen Lemmel (1918); Lemmel, Helen Lemmel (1922)

"The Solid Rock/My Hope Is Built on Nothing Less"—Edward Mote (1834); Solid Rock, William Bradbury (1863)

WHEN IS EASTER?

Easter Sunday is the Sunday following the first full moon of spring, known as the Paschal Full Moon.

In June 325 CE, astronomers estimated astronomical full-moon dates for the church, calling them Ecclesiastical Full Moon dates. Since 326, the Paschal Full Moon date has always been the Ecclesiastical Full Moon date after March 20 (the equinox date in 325). According to these calculations, the earliest possible date for Easter is March 22 and the latest April 25.

TEN MAJOR DISCOVERIES IN BIBLICAL ARCHAEOLOGY

1. The Nag Hammadi Library
   In 1945 two peasants discovered a thirteen-volume library of Coptic texts hidden under a boulder near the town of Nag Hammadi in upper Egypt. This reintroduced the largely forgotten Gnostic strain of early Christianity.

2. 'Ain Dara Temple
   This temple in northern Syria is the most similar known structure to Solomon's temple. Its plan, size, date, and architectural details are typical of sacred architecture of the area between the tenth and the eighth centuries BCE.

3. Tel Dan ("David") Stela
   This ninth-century BCE inscription provides the first evidence for King David outside the Bible.

4. "Mona Lisa of Galilee"
   More than sixteen centuries after an earthquake destroyed the Roman city of Sepphoris, just west of the Sea of Galilee, this richly colored mosaic portrait of an unnamed woman was discovered among the ruins.

5. "Peter's House"
   This simple first-century CE home in Capernaum may have been occupied by Jesus during his Galilean ministry. It seems subsequently to have become a place for communal—possibly Christian—gatherings linked with Jesus and his disciple Peter.

6. The Siloam Pool
   In 2004, archaeologists excavated part of this monumental pool south of Jerusalem's Temple Mount, on the ridge known as the City of David, where Jesus restored the sight of a blind man in John's Gospel.

7. Ashkelon's Arched Gate
   This is the oldest known monumental arch, built during the Middle Bronze Age, circa 1850 BCE, and discovered in southern Israel in 1992. During the same dig, a beautiful silver calf statuette was also found.

8. The Dead Sea Scrolls
   This hugely important library of more than eight hundred manuscripts dating from between circa 250 BCE and 68 CE,

discovered in 1947 by a Bedouin shepherd in caves near the Dead Sea, affords unique insights into contemporary Judaism and religious culture, and the Bible before the canon was established in the second century CE.

9. Jerusalem Siege Tower and Arrowheads
Uncovered during excavations in Jerusalem's Jewish Quarter during the 1970s, this twenty-two-foot tower, with walls twelve feet thick, formed part of Jerusalem's defenses against the Babylonian invasion of 586 BCE. A thick layer of charred wood, ashes, and soot around its base is evidence of the fire that accompanied the Babylonian destruction. In the rubble, excavators discovered five arrowheads—four of iron, as utilized by the Israelites, and one of bronze, which is typical of the Babylonian army.

10. Siloam Inscription in "Hezekiah's Tunnel," Jerusalem
Discovered by two boys playing in the tunnel in 1880, the inscription describes the moment when quarrymen from each end met in the middle, possibly throwing light on 2 Kings 20:20.

NICKNAMES FOR BIBLE VERSIONS

These monikers are mainly used by critics of these versions.

Always Superior Version: American Standard Version (ASV)
Close Enough Version: Contemporary English Version (CEV)
Eliminated Scriptures Version: English Standard Version (ESV)—it omits Bible verses
Error Saturated Version: English Standard Version (ESV)
Gender Neutered Bible: Good News Bible (GNB)—it is marked by excessive gender-inclusivity
Near Enough Bible: New English Bible (NEB)
Nearly Infallible Version: New International Version (NIV)
New Age Standard Bible: New American Standard Bible (NASB)
New Incorrect Version: New International Version (NIV)

New Liberal Translation: New Living Translation (NLT)

New Reprobate Standard Version: New Revised Standard Version (NRSV)

North American (Southern Californian) Bible: New American Standard Bible (NASB)

Not Always the Same Before: New American Standard Bible (NASB)—it boasted copyright revisions in 1960, 1962, 1963, 1968, 1971, 1972, 1973, 1975, 1977, and 1995

Not a Solid Bible: New American Standard Bible (NASB)

Not Racist/Sexist Version: New Revised Standard Version (NRSV)—it omits racist and sexist language

Really Silly Version: Revised Standard Version (RSV)

Retro-Sounding Version: Revised Standard Version (RSV)

The Mess: The Message paraphrase, by Eugene Peterson

Totally Non-Inspired Version: Today's New International Version (TNIV)

"LIGHTEN OUR DARKNESS"

Lighten our darkness, we beseech thee, O Lord;
and by thy great mercy defend us
from all perils and dangers of this night;
for the love of thy only Son, our Savior, Jesus Christ.

—*Book of Common Prayer*

"FOR I WILL CONSIDER MY CAT JEOFFRY"

Written in part while the poet was confined at St. Luke's Hospital for Lunatics, London.

For I will consider my Cat Jeoffry.
For he is the servant of the Living God duly and daily serving him.
For at the first glance of the glory of God in the East he worships in his way.

For this is done by wreathing his body seven times round with elegant quickness.
For then he leaps up to catch the musk, which is the blessing of God upon his prayer.
For he rolls upon prank to work it in.
For having done duty and received blessing he begins to consider himself.
For this he performs in ten degrees.
For first he looks upon his fore-paws to see if they are clean.
For secondly he kicks up behind to clear away there.
For thirdly he works it upon stretch with the fore-paws extended.
For fourthly he sharpens his paws by wood.
For fifthly he washes himself.
For sixthly he rolls upon wash.
For seventhly he fleas himself, that he may not be interrupted upon the beat.
For eighthly he rubs himself against a post.
For ninthly he looks up for his instructions.
For tenthly he goes in quest of food.
For having consider'd God and himself he will consider his neighbor.
For if he meets another cat he will kiss her in kindness.
For when he takes his prey he plays with it to give it a chance.
For one mouse in seven escapes by his dallying.
For when his day's work is done his business more properly begins.
For he keeps the Lord's watch in the night against the adversary. . . .
For he purrs in thankfulness, when God tells him he's a good Cat.
For he is an instrument for the children to learn benevolence upon.
For every house is incomplete without him and a blessing is lacking in the spirit.

For the Lord commanded Moses concerning the cats at the
    departure of the Children of Israel from Egypt. . . .
For he knows that God is his Savior.
For there is nothing sweeter than his peace when at rest.
For there is nothing brisker than his life when in motion.
For he is of the Lord's poor and so indeed is he called by
    benevolence perpetually—Poor Jeoffry! poor Jeoffry! the
    rat has bit thy throat.
For I bless the name of the Lord Jesus that Jeoffry is better.
For the divine spirit comes about his body to sustain it in
    complete cat.

—from Jubilate Agno,
Christopher Smart (1722–1771), English poet

"OUR LAST AWAKENING"

Bring us, O Lord God, at our last awakening
into the house and gate of heaven,
to enter into that gate and dwell in that house,
where there shall be no darkness nor dazzling, but one
    equal light;
no noise nor silence, but one equal music;
no fears nor hopes, but one equal possession;
no ends nor beginnings, but one equal eternity:
in the habitations of thy majesty and glory,
world without end.

—John Donne (1572–1631), English writer

"THE LATEST DECALOGUE"

An English poet critiques the morality of Victorian society:

Thou shalt have one God only; who
Would be at the expense of two?
No graven images may be
Worshipped, except the currency:

Swear not at all; for, for thy curse
Thine enemy is none the worse:
At church on Sunday to attend
Will serve to keep the world thy friend:
Honor thy parents; that is, all
From whom advancement may befall:
Thou shalt not kill; but need'st not strive
Officiously to keep alive:
Do not adultery commit;
Advantage rarely comes of it:
Thou shalt not steal; an empty feat,
When it's so lucrative to cheat:
Bear not false witness; let the lie
Have time on its own wings to fly:
Thou shalt not covet; but tradition
Approves all forms of competition.

The sum of all is, thou shalt love,
If anybody, God above:
At any rate shall never labour
More than thyself to love thy neighbour.

—*Arthur Hugh Clough (1819–1861), English poet*

SOMETHING ETERNAL

Now there are some things we all know, but we don't take'm out and look at'm very often. We all know that something is eternal. And it ain't houses and it ain't names, and it ain't earth, and it ain't even the stars . . . everybody knows in their bones that something is eternal, and that something has to do with human beings. All the greatest people ever lived have been telling us that for five thousand years, and yet you'd be surprised how people are always losing hold of it. There's something way down deep that's eternal about every human being.

—*from* Our Town, *Thornton Wilder (1897–1975),*
American playwright

FIRE

Blaise Pascal, the seventeenth-century scholar, experienced a dramatic conversion following a mystical experience. After his vision, he wrote a record that he sewed into his jacket and was discovered only after his death.

> The year of grace 1654,
> Monday, 23 November, feast of St. Clement, pope and martyr, and others in the martyrology.
> Vigil of St. Chrysogonus, martyr, and others.
> From about half-past ten at night until about half-past midnight,
> FIRE.
> GOD of Abraham, GOD of Isaac, GOD of Jacob
> not of the philosophers and of the savants.
> Certitude. Certitude. Feeling. Joy. Peace.
> GOD of Jesus Christ.
> My God and your God.
> "Your GOD shall be my God."
> Forgetfulness of the world and of everything, except GOD.
> He is only found in the ways taught in the gospel.
> Grandeur of the human soul.
> Righteous Father, the world has not known you, but I have known you.
> Joy, joy, joy, tears of joy.
> I have departed from him:
> "They have forsaken me, the fount of living water."
> My God, will you forsake me?
> Let me not be separated from him forever.
> This is life eternal, that they know you, the one true God, and the one that you sent, Jesus Christ.
> Jesus Christ.
> Jesus Christ.
> I have fallen away; I fled him, renounced him, crucified him.

Let me never be separated from him.
We hold him, only kept by the ways taught in the gospel:
Renunciation, total and sweet.
Complete submission to Jesus Christ and to my director.
Eternally in Joy for a day's exercise on the earth.
May I not forget your word.
Amen.

THE GENERAL CONFESSION

Almighty and most merciful Father, We have erred, and strayed from thy ways like lost sheep, We have followed too much the devices and desires of our own hearts, We have offended against thy holy laws, We have left undone those things which we ought to have done, And we have done those things which we ought not to have done, And there is no health in us: But thou, O Lord, have mercy upon us miserable offenders; Spare thou them, O God, which confess their faults, Restore thou them that are penitent, According to thy promises declared unto mankind in Christ Jesu our Lord: And grant, O most merciful Father, for his sake, That we may hereafter live a godly, righteous, and sober life, To the glory of thy holy Name. Amen.

—*Book of Common Prayer*

"IN THE BLEAK MIDWINTER"

In the bleak midwinter, frosty wind made moan,
Earth stood hard as iron, water like a stone;
Snow had fallen, snow on snow, snow on snow,
In the bleak midwinter, long ago.

Our God, heaven cannot hold him, nor earth sustain;
Heaven and earth shall flee away when he comes to reign.

In the bleak midwinter a stable place sufficed
The Lord God Almighty, Jesus Christ.

Enough for him, whom cherubim worship night and day,
A breastful of milk and a mangerful of hay;
Enough for him, whom angels fall down before,
The ox and ass and camel which adore.

Angels and archangels may have gathered there,
Cherubim and seraphim thronged the air;
But only his mother, in her maiden bliss,
Worshipped the beloved with a kiss.

What can I give him, poor as I am?
If I were a shepherd, I would bring a lamb;
If I were a Wise Man, I would do my part;
Yet what I can I give him: give him my heart.

—*Christina Rossetti (1830–1894), English poet*

GOSSE'S CHRISTMAS

Edmund Gosse describes Christmas Day with his Plymouth Brethren father, the naturalist Philip Gosse.

> On the subject of all feasts of the Church [my father] held views of an almost grotesque peculiarity. He looked upon each of them as nugatory and worthless, but the keeping of Christmas appeared to him by far the most hateful, and nothing less than an act of idolatry. "The very word is Popish," he used to exclaim, "Christ's Mass!" pursing up his lips. . . . Then he would adduce the antiquity of the so-called feast, adapted from horrible heathen rites, and itself a soiled relic of the abominable Yule-Tide. He would denounce the horrors of Christmas until it almost made me blush to look at a holly-berry.

On Christmas Day of this year 1857 our villa saw a very unusual sight. My father had given strictest charge that no difference whatever was to be made in our meals on that day; the dinner was to be neither more copious than usual nor less so. He was obeyed, but the servants, secretly rebellious, made a small plum-pudding for themselves. . . . Early in the afternoon, the maids—of whom we were now advanced to keeping two—kindly remarked that "the poor dear child ought to have a bit, anyhow," and wheedled me into the kitchen, where I ate a slice of plum-pudding. Shortly I began to feel that pain inside which in my frail state was inevitable, and my conscience smote me violently. At length I could bear my spiritual anguish no longer, and bursting into the study I called out: "Oh! Papa, Papa, I have eaten of flesh offered to idols!" It took some time, between my sobs, to explain what had happened. Then my Father sternly said: "Where is the accursed thing?" I explained that as much as was left of it was still on the kitchen table. He took me by the hand, and ran with me into the midst of the startled servants, seized what remained of the pudding, and with the plate in one hand and me still tight in the other, ran till we reached the dust-heap, when he flung the idolatrous confectionery on to the middle of the ashes, and then raked it deep down into the mass. The suddenness, the violence, the velocity of this extraordinary act made an impression on my memory which nothing will ever efface.

—*from* Father and Son, *Edmund Gosse (1849–1928),*
English writer

"UPON CHRIST HIS BIRTH"

Strange news! a city full? will none give way
To lodge a guest that comes not every day?
No inn, nor tavern void? yet I descry
One empty place alone, where we may lie:

> In too much fullness is some want: but where?
> Men's empty hearts: let's ask for lodging there.
> But if they not admit us, then we'll say
> Their hearts, as well as inns, are made of clay.
>
> —*Sir John Suckling (1609–1641), English Cavalier poet*

"THE FIRST BLAST OF THE TRUMPET AGAINST THE MONSTROUS REGIMENT OF WOMEN"

A misogynistic polemic against women rulers.

> To promote a Woman to beare rule, superioritie, dominion, or empire above any Realme, nation, or Citie, is repugnant to Nature; contumelie to God, a thing most contrarious to his reveled will and approved ordinance; and finallie, it is the subversion of good Order, of all equitie and justice.... For who can denie but it is repugneth to nature, that the blind shall be appointed to leade and conduct such as do see? That the weake, the sicke, and impotent persons shall norishe and kepe the hole and strong? And finallie, that the foolishe, madde, and phrenetike shal governe the discrete, and give counsel to such as the sober of mind? And such be al women, compared unto man in bearing of authoritie. For their sight in civile regiment is but blindnes; their strength, weaknes; their counsel, foolishnes; and judgment, phrensie, if it be rightlie considered.
>
> ... Nature, I say, doth paynt them further to be weake, fraile, impacient, feble, and foolishe; and experience hath declared them to be unconstant, variable, cruell, and lacking the spirit of counsel and regiment.
>
> —*John Knox (c. 1514–1572), Scots reformer*

An Englishman responds:

> If nature hath given it them by birth, how dare we pull it from them by violence? If God have called them to it, either

to save or to spill, why should we repine at that which is God's will and order? Are we . . . so bold to alter that [which] He purpose should come of it? If He able women, shall we unable them? If He meant not that they should minister, He could have provided other. Therefore the safest way is to let Him do His will. . . . It is a plain argument that for some secret purpose He mindeth the female should reign and govern.

> —from "An Harborowe for Faithfull and
> Trewe Subjectes, against the late blowne Blaste,
> concerning the Government of Wemen, wherin
> be confuted all such reasons as a straunger of late
> made in that behalfe, with a briefe exhortation
> to Obedience 1559," John Aylmer (1521–1594),
> English bishop

CHOSEN?

A TWELVE-YEAR-OLD WRITES TO HIS PURITAN FATHER:

Though I am thus well in body yet I question whether my soul doth prosper as my body doth, for I perceive yet to this very day, little growth in grace; and this makes me question whether grace be in my heart or no. I feel also daily great unwillingness to good duties, and the great ruling of sin in my heart; and that God is angry with me and gives me no answers to my prayers; but many times he even throws them down as dust in my face; and he does not grant my continued request for the spiritual blessing of the softening of my hard heart. And in all this I could yet take some comfort but that it makes me to wonder what God's secret decree concerning me may be: for I doubt whether even God is wont to deny grace and mercy to his chosen (though uncalled) when they seek unto him by prayer for it; and therefore, seeing he doth thus deny it to me, I think that the reason of it is most like to be because I belong not unto the election of grace. I desire that you would let me have your prayers as I doubt not but I have them, and rest

Your Son,
Samuel Mather

—Samuel Mather (1626–1671), independent clergyman. Samuel's father, Richard Mather, took him from Lancashire, England, to New England, where he was educated at Harvard College.

WESTMINSTER SHORTER CATECHISM

This catechism was written to educate children and others "of weaker capacity" in the Reformed faith. Here are its first ten questions.

Q. 1. What is the chief end of man?
A. Man's chief end is to glorify God, and to enjoy him forever.

Q. 2. What rule hath God given to direct us how we may glorify and enjoy him?
A. The Word of God, which is contained in the Scriptures of the Old and New Testaments, is the only rule to direct us how we may glorify and enjoy him.

Q. 3. What do the Scriptures principally teach?
A. The Scriptures principally teach, what man is to believe concerning God, and what duty God requires of man.

Q. 4. What is God?
A. God is a Spirit, infinite, eternal, and unchangeable, in his being, wisdom, power, holiness, justice, goodness, and truth.

Q. 5. Are there more Gods than one?
A. There is but one only, the living and true God.

Q. 6. How many persons are there in the Godhead?

A. There are three persons in the Godhead: the Father, the Son, and the Holy Ghost; and these three are one God, the same in substance, equal in power and glory.

Q. 7. What are the decrees of God?

A. The decrees of God are his eternal purpose, according to the counsel of his will, whereby, for his own glory, he hath foreordained whatsoever comes to pass.

Q. 8. How doth God execute his decrees?

A. God executeth his decrees in the works of creation and providence.

Q. 9. What is the work of creation?

A. The work of creation is, God's making all things of nothing, by the word of his power, in the space of six days, and all very good.

Q. 10. How did God create man?

A. God created man male and female, after his own image, in knowledge, righteousness, and holiness, with dominion over the creatures. . . .

—London, 1646–1647

JESUS'S PARABLES IN MATTHEW, MARK, AND LUKE

The Synoptic Gospels—Matthew, Mark, and Luke—contain much similar material, including the parables told by Jesus. However, every parable is not found in all the Gospels.

Only in Mark

The seed growing in secret (Mark 4:26–29)

Only in Matthew

The weeds among the wheat (Matt. 13:24-30)
The hidden treasure (13:44)
The pearl of great value (13:45-46)
The dragnet (13:47-50)
The unforgiving servant (18:23-35)
The laborers in the vineyard (20:1-16)
The two sons (21:28-31)
The ten bridesmaids (25:1-12)
The talents (25:14-30)

Only in Luke

The two debtors (Luke 7:41-42)
The good Samaritan (10:30-37)
The rich fool (12:16-21)
The lost coin (15:8-10)
The prodigal and his brother (15:11-32)
The dishonest manager (16:1-8)
The rich man and Lazarus (16:19-31)

In Matthew and Luke but Not in Mark

The yeast (Matt. 13:33; Luke 13:20-21)
The lost sheep (Matt. 18:12-14; Luke 15:3-7)
The great dinner (Matt. 22:1-14; Luke 14:15-24)

In Mark, Matthew, and Luke

The sower (Mark 4:1-20; Matt. 13:3-23; Luke 8:5-15)
The mustard seed (Mark 4:30-32; Matt. 13:31-32; Luke 13:18-19)
The wicked tenants (Mark 12:1-11; Matt. 21:33-46; Luke 20:9-18)
The fig tree (Mark 13:28-32; Matt. 24:32-36; Luke 21:29-33)
The faithful slave (Mark 13:33-37; Matt. 24:42; Luke 12:35-48)

MORE SCRIPTURE UNAWARES

Here are some commonplace words and phrases from the King James Version of the New Testament:

Salt of the earth	Matthew 5:13
No man can serve two masters	Matthew 6:24
Pearls before swine	Matthew 7:6
The blind lead the blind	Matthew 15:14
Signs of the times	Matthew 16:3
The last shall be first	Matthew 20:16
Many are called, but few are chosen	Matthew 22:14
Good and faithful servant	Matthew 25:21
Physician, heal thyself	Luke 4:23
Eat, drink, and be merry	Luke 12:19
What I have written I have written	John 19:22
Turned the world upside down	Acts 17:6
A law unto themselves	Romans 2:14
Vengeance is mine	Romans 12:19
The powers that be	Romans 13:1
All things to all men	1 Corinthians 9:22
Through a glass, darkly	1 Corinthians 13:12
In the twinkling of an eye	1 Corinthians 15:52
Suffer fools gladly	2 Corinthians 11:19
A thorn in the flesh	2 Corinthians 12:7
Fallen from grace	Galatians 5:4
Filthy lucre	1 Timothy 3:8
Fight the good fight	1 Timothy 6:12
The patience of Job	James 5:11

"E TENEBRIS"

Come down, O Christ, and help me! reach thy hand,
For I am drowning in a stormier sea
Than Simon on thy lake of Galilee:

The wine of life is spilt upon the sand,
My heart is in some famine-murdered land
Whence all good things have perished utterly,
And well I know my soul in Hell must lie
If I this night before God's throne should stand.
"He sleeps perchance, or rideth to the chase,
Like Baal, when his prophets howled that name
From morn to noon on Carmel's smitten height."
Nay, peace, I shall behold, before the night,
The feet of brass, the robe more white than flame,
The wounded hands, the weary human face.

—*Oscar Wilde (1854–1900), Irish playwright*

INKLING WISDOM

Quotations from C. S. Lewis, Christian apologist and author of the Narnia chronicles.

> No man knows how bad he is till he has tried very hard to be good.
>
> —*Mere Christianity*

> Miracles are a retelling in small letters of the very same story which is written across the whole world in letters too large for some of us to see.
>
> —*God in the Dock*

> If I find in myself desires which nothing in this world can satisfy, the only logical explanation is that I was made for another world.
>
> —*Mere Christianity*

> God whispers to us in our pleasures, speaks to us in our conscience, but shouts in our pains; it is his megaphone to rouse a deaf world.
>
> —*The Problem of Pain*

If God forgives us we must forgive ourselves. Otherwise it's like setting up ourselves as a higher tribunal than him.

—*Collected Letters of C. S. Lewis*

Everyone says forgiveness is a lovely idea, until they have something to forgive.

—*Mere Christianity*

Once in our world, a stable had something in it that was bigger than our whole world.

—*The Last Battle*

To be a Christian means to forgive the inexcusable, because God has forgiven the inexcusable in you.

—*Essays on Forgiveness*

The Son of God became a man to enable men to become sons of God.

—*Mere Christianity*

BAD POPES

During the ninth and tenth centuries and the Renaissance, corruption flourished in the Vatican.

- *Stephen VI* (896–897): At the "Cadaver Synod" of January 897, Stephen VI dug up a hated predecessor, Pope Formosus (891–896), clothed his mummified corpse in papal robes, placed it on the throne, and tried it. When the corpse was (inevitably) found guilty, Stephen cut off the three fingers Formosus had used in blessing and tossed them into the Tiber River.
- *John XII* (r. 955–964): Elected pope at the age of eighteen, John XII allegedly had sex with both women and men in the papal palace, which was described as a "brothel." One account claims John XII was murdered by a cuckolded husband—another that, aged only twenty-seven, he died of a stroke in bed

with a married woman. He was also accused of ordaining a ten-year-old as bishop.

Benedict IX (r. 1032–1048): Becoming pontiff at around twenty years old and still a layman, Benedict IX was accused of rape, adultery, and murder; his carousing eventually resulted in expulsion from Rome. After he managed to regain his throne, with the support of his family's private army, he sold the papacy to his godfather, John Gratian, who named himself Gregory VI.

Alexander VI (r. 1492–1503): The infamous Rodrigo Borgia flaunted his young mistress in the Vatican and is alleged to have poisoned cardinals. When elected to the papacy, he was already father, by three different women, to eight children, for whom he organized dynastic marriages with powerful princes. The preacher Girolamo Savonarola (1452–1498) attacked Alexander's papacy as a "prostitute church."

Paul III (r. 1534–1549): Alessandro Farnese, when a cardinal, kept a mistress, by whom he had four children; his two teenage grandsons were the first cardinals he appointed after achieving the papacy. Paul III staged lavish entertainments, including bullfights and horse races, for the citizens of Rome, and his decisions were frequently arrived at by astrology.

Julius III (r. 1550–1555): Picked up a teenaged beggar called Innocenzo in a Parma street and adopted him as his "nephew." When he became pope, Julius made him a cardinal, showering lavish gifts upon him. Julius spent much of the papal finances renovating his mansion, the splendid Villa Giulia, where he staged extravagant entertainments.

SONNET 19

When I consider how my light is spent,
   Ere half my days, in this dark world and wide,
   And that one talent which is death to hide
   Lodged with me useless, though my soul more bent
To serve therewith my Maker, and present

> My true account, lest he returning chide,
> "Doth God exact day-labor, light denied?"
> I fondly ask. But Patience, to prevent
> That murmur, soon replies, "God doth not need
> Either man's work or his own gifts; who best
> Bear his mild yoke, they serve him best. His state
> Is kingly: thousands at his bidding speed,
> And post o'er land and ocean without rest:
> They also serve who only stand and wait."
>
> —*John Milton (1608-1674), English poet*

MONASTIC ORDERS

Following are some monastic orders and their popular names.

Benedictines: Order of St. Benedict, founded by Benedict of Nursia, c. 529, a.k.a. Black Monks, for their black habit

Bonhommes: Brothers of Penitence, a.k.a. Friars of the Sack, Blue Friars

Bridgettines: founded by St. Bridget of Sweden, 1344

Camaldolites, Camaldolese: founded by Romuald at Camaldoli, Italy, c. 1012

Capuchins: Friars Minor Capuchin, a branch of the Franciscans. "Cappuccino coffee" is the color of the Capuchin hood.

Carmelites: Order of the Brothers of the Blessed Virgin Mary of Mount Carmel, or White Friars, founded in the twelfth century

Carthusians: founded at Chartreuse, France, 1084; a.k.a. Order of St. Bruno

Catholic sisters of the Servants of the Immaculate Heart of Mary, a.k.a. Blue Nuns

Christian Brothers: the Congregation of Christian Brothers, founded by Edmund Rice, 1802

Cistercians: founded at Cîteaux Abbey, France, 1098

Conventual Franciscans: branch of Franciscans, a.k.a. Minorites, or Grey Friars; formed by Francis of Assisi, 1209

Culdees (from the Irish: *Céilí Dé* = "Spouses of God"): medieval British communities of monks and hermits

Dominicans: mendicants founded by Dominic de Gúzman, 1216, a.k.a. Friars Preacher, Black Friars

Franciscans: Order of Friars Minor, or Observants, founded by Francis of Assisi, 1209

Gilbertines: Order of Canons Regular, founded by Gilbert of Sempringham, c. 1130

Hospitallers: the Order of Knights of the Hospital of St. John of Jerusalem, founded 1070

Ignorantines: founded by the Abbé de la Salle in 1724, to educate poor children

Jesuits: the Society of Jesus, founded by Ignatius Loyola, 1540

Knights Templar: Poor Fellow-Soldiers of Christ and of the Temple of Solomon, founded 1119

Minims: order of friars founded by St. Francis of Paola, 1435

Norbertines: Canons Regular of Prémontré, or Premonstratensians, founded by Norbert of Xanten, 1120

Oratorians: Congregation of the Oratory of Philip Neri, founded 1575

Poor Clares, or Second Order of the Friars Minor: founded by Clare of Assisi and Francis of Assisi, 1212

Salesians: Salesians of Don Bosco, founded by John Bosco, 1859

Theatines: Congregation of Clerics Regular of the Divine Providence, founded by St. Cajetan, 1524

Trappists: Order of Cistercians of the Strict Observance, founded by Armand Jean le Bouthillier de Rancé, 1664

Visitandines: the Order of the Visitation of Holy Mary, founded by St. Francis de Sales and St. Jane Frances de Chantal, 1610

SOME FICTIONAL LIVES OF JESUS

The gospel story and the figure of Christ have fascinated many authors.

Lew Wallace: *Ben-Hur: A Tale of the Christ* (1880)
Henry Sienkiewicz: *Quo Vadis?* (1896)

Sholem Asch: *The Nazarene* (1939)
Lloyd C. Douglas: *The Robe* (1942)
Robert Graves: *King Jesus* (1946)
Nikos Kazantzakis: *The Last Temptation of Christ* (1960)
Marjorie Holmes: *Two from Galilee* (1972)
Norman Mailer: *The Gospel according to the Son* (1997)
Walter Wangerin: *Jesus: A Novel* (2005)
Anne Rice: *Christ the Lord: Out of Egypt* (2005)
Philip Pullman: *The Good Man Jesus and the Scoundrel Christ* (2010)
Colm Tóibín: *The Testament of Mary* (2012)
Naomi Alderman: *The Liars' Gospel* (2012)

"CROSSING THE BAR"

Sunset and evening star,
    And one clear call for me!
And may there be no moaning of the bar,
    When I put out to sea,

But such a tide as moving seems asleep,
    Too full for sound and foam,
When that which drew from out the boundless deep
    Turns again home.

Twilight and evening bell,
    And after that the dark!
And may there be no sadness of farewell,
    When I embark;

For tho' from out our bourne of Time and Place
    The flood may bear me far,
I hope to see my Pilot face to face
    When I have crost the bar.

—Alfred, Lord Tennyson (1809–1892), English poet

THE BAREBONE FAMILY

Sounding like characters from a horror movie, the Barebones were seventeenth-century English Puritans with a propensity for striking names. They included two sets of brothers:

Praise-God Barebone
Fear-God Barebone
Jesus-Christ-came-into-the-world-to-save Barebone
If-Christ-had-not-Died-for-thee-thou-hadst-been-damned Barebone

The contemporary dramatist Ben Jonson satirized Puritans with such characters as Zeal-of-the-Land Busy, who stops a puppet show by claiming it amounts to idol worship.

TERRIBLE RELIGIOUS JOKES

If you laugh at these, you'll laugh at anything.

How does Moses make tea?
He brews it.

What happened when Moses had a headache?
God gave him the tablets.

Who is the biggest lawbreaker in the Bible?
Moses broke all ten commandments at the same time.

What did Moses say when he saw people worshiping the golden calf?
Holy cow!

Who is the first tennis player in the Bible?
Joseph, who served in Pharaoh's court

Who's the best comedian in the Bible?
Samson: he brought the house down.

How do angels greet each other?
Halo, halo, halo!

How do you make God laugh?
Tell him your plans.

Why are atoms Catholic?
Because they have mass.

A rabbi, a priest, and a minister walk into a bar.
The bartender looks up and says, "What is this—a joke?"

CHURCHY WORDS

A brief vocabulary relating to church buildings:

> *Altar*: main table at front of church where the bread and wine are blessed during the Eucharist. It can be wooden, concrete, or marble. In old churches, there may be a screen or altarpiece behind it.
> *Ambo*: speaker's podium
> *Ambry*: box in which three holy oils are stored
> *Ambulatory*: walkway inside or outside a church. If outdoors, it may be a cloister—a courtyard of columns or arches.
> *Apse*: semicircular or polygonal space where the altar is located
> *Baldachino*: cover or sounding board over a pulpit
> *Chancel*: area between the congregation and the sanctuary, where clergy and/or choir sit.
> *Cloister*: an outdoor courtyard of columns or arches
> *Confessional*: enclosed cabinet where Catholics confess their sins to a priest
> *Crossing*: place where the nave, chancel, and transept intersect

Crucifix: cross bearing image of Jesus

Font: stone bowl used to baptize babies

Lectern: stand from which the Bible is read

Monstrance: ornate vessel used to contain the consecrated Eucharist

Nave (from *navis*, Latin for ship): area where congregation sit or stand. In many Eastern Catholic and Orthodox churches, congregants stand during the liturgy

Pulpit: raised desk from which priest delivers sermon. Not all churches have both lectern and pulpit; some have only a speaker's podium, or ambo.

Relic: bone or other remnant of a saint

Reredos: ornate altarpiece

Sacristy, or vestry: place for storing religious vestments and liturgical vessels

Sanctuary: place where the tabernacle is located. In Catholic churches, it is marked by a permanent light.

Sanctuary, or paschal, candle: candle that signifies the presence of Christ

Stained glass windows: windows made of colored glass on which stories from the Bible or portraits of saints are depicted

Stoup: small basin containing holy water, which is used to make the sign of the cross

Tabernacle: locked box where leftover eucharistic elements are stored

Transept: transverse arm of a cruciform church

SOME ARCHBISHOPS OF CANTERBURY

Augustine	597–604/5	first archbishop
Deusdedit	655–664	first English archbishop
Wighard	664	died of plague before being consecrated
Adrian	664	appointed by the pope but turned it down

Beorhtweald	693–731	
Ethelhard	793–805	
Aelfheah (Alphege)	1006–1012	killed by the Danes
Thomas Becket	1162–1170	murdered
Baldwin	1185–1190	died on Crusade
Simon Sudbury	1375–1381	beheaded by Wat Tyler's rebels
Thomas Arundel	1396–1397	charged with high treason and fled (later restored)
Thomas Cranmer	1533–1556	burnt at the stake during the reign of Mary Tudor
William Laud	1633–1645	executed during Interregnum

A LONG WAIT

In the old days, somewhere in eastern Europe, a traveler arrived in a *shtetl* in the middle of winter. There, outside the synagogue, an old man sat on a bench, shivering in the cold.

"What are you doing here?" asked the traveler.

"I'm waiting for the coming of Messiah."

"That is indeed a very important job," said the traveler. "I suppose the community pays you a good salary?"

"No, not at all," said the old man. "They don't pay me anything. They just let me sit on this bench. Once in a while someone comes out and gives me a little food."

"That must be very hard for you," said the traveler. "But even if they don't pay you anything, surely they must honor you for undertaking this important task?"

"No, not at all," said the old man. "They all think that I'm crazy."

"I don't understand this," said the traveler. "They don't pay you. They don't respect you. You sit out here in the cold, shivering, hungry. What kind of a job is this?"

The old man replied: "It's *steady work*."

LUTHER ON RELICS

Luther satirized relics exhibited for indulgences, including:

> Three flames from the burning bush on Mount Sinai
> A whole pound of wind that roared by Elijah in the cave on Mount Horeb
> Five nice strings from the harp of David
> Three beautiful locks of Absalom's hair, which got caught in the oak and left him hanging
> A morsel of bread from the Last Supper
> Two feathers and an egg from the Holy Spirit

"ADDRESS TO THE DEVIL"

> Satan, I fear thy sooty claws
> An' now, Auld Cloots,
> I ken ye're thinkin,
> A certain Bardie's rantin, drinkin,
> Some luckless hour will send him linkin
> To your black pit:
> But, faith! He'll turn a corner jinkin,
> An' cheat you yet.
>
> —*Robert Burns (1759–1796), Scottish poet*

PATRIOTISM IS NOT ENOUGH

> O Lord our Father, our young patriots, idols of our hearts, go forth to battle—be Thou near them! With them, in spirit, we also go forth from the sweet peace of our beloved firesides to smite the foe. O Lord our God, help us to tear their soldiers to bloody shreds with our shells; help us to cover their smiling fields with the pale forms of their patriot dead;

help us to drown the thunder of the guns with the shrieks of their wounded, writhing in pain; help us to lay waste their humble homes with a hurricane of fire; help us to wring the hearts of their unoffending widows with unavailing grief; help us to turn them out roofless with their little children to wander unfriended the wastes of their desolated land in rags and hunger and thirst . . . Lord, blast their hopes, blight their lives, protract their bitter pilgrimage, make heavy their steps, water their way with their tears, stain the white snow with the blood of their wounded feet! We ask it, in the spirit of love, of Him Who is the Source of Love, and Who is everfaithful refuge and friend of all that are sore beset and seek His aid with humble and contrite hearts. Amen.

—*Mark Twain (1835–1910), American author*

HYPOCRISY

If the Bible is universally diffused in Hindustan, what must be the astonishment of the natives to find that we are forbidden to rob, murder and steal; we who, in fifty years, have extended our empire . . . and exemplified in our public conduct every crime of which human nature is capable. What matchless impudence to follow up such practice with such precepts! If we have common prudence, let us keep the gospel at home, and tell them that Machiavelli is our prophet, and the god of the Manicheans our god.

—*Sir Sidney Smith (1764–1840), British naval officer*

LAUGHING IN CHURCH

If someone is coughing and doesn't sing well at the start of the psalms, he is to be punished with six strokes. . . . Anyone who smiles during the service will also receive six strokes;

and anyone who breaks into noisy laughter will be deprived of food, unless he has some acceptable excuse.

—from St. Columban's monastic rule,
Regula Coenobialis

TEN FACTS ABOUT THE DEAD SEA SCROLLS

Since they were first discovered in 1947, these ancient documents have been shrouded in mystery and controversy.

1. Esther is the only Old Testament book *not* found in the scrolls. Most of the scrolls are nonbiblical writings, but two hundred are copies of Old Testament books.

2. There may be hidden treasure . . .
    The Copper Scroll lists sixty-three locations containing gold or silver—though none has been discovered.

3. Some scrolls were phylacteries—tiny pieces of parchment worn by Jewish men, containing verses from the Torah: Exodus 13:9, Exodus 13:16, Deuteronomy 6:8, Deuteronomy 11:18.

4. The Isaiah scroll—estimated as between 2,350 and 2,100 years old—is 1,000 years older than any previously known Hebrew copy of the book.

5. The scrolls were in three different languages: 75 percent in Hebrew; most of the rest in Aramaic; a small number in Greek.

6. The Temple Scroll—the longest—was 26.7 feet long and describes the construction of an ideal temple.

7. The fourth cave (of eleven) contained 90 percent of the total hoard: 15,000 fragments from 500 scrolls.

8. Scholars do not know with any certainty who wrote the scrolls: the best conjecture is the Essene sect of Jews—or possibly the Sadducees.

9. More significant documents are written on goat and calf hides, considered "purer" than other animals.

10. As recently as 2018, one of two remaining unpublished scrolls was decoded.

TEN NOVELS ABOUT KING DAVID

Juan Bosch, *David: Biography of a King* (1966)
Stefan Heym, *The King David Report* (1972)
Malachi Martin, *King of Kings* (1980)
Joseph Heller, *God Knows* (1984)
Madeleine L'Engle, *Certain Women* (1993)
Allan Massie, *King David* (1995)
Yochi Brandes, *The Secret Book of Kings* (2008)
Geraldine Brooks, *The Secret Chord* (2015)
Paul Boorstin, *David and the Philistine Woman* (2017)
Michael Arditti, *The Anointed* (2020)

SOURCES

Translated quotations are drawn from the following sources.

Acts of Paul and Thecla. In *Apocryphal Gospels, Acts, and Revelations.* Vol. 16 of *The Ante-Nicene Christian Library*. Edited by Alexander Roberts and James Donaldson. Translated by Alexander Walker. Edinburgh: T&T Clark, 1873.

Augustine of Hippo. *The Confessions of St. Augustine, Bishop of Hippo.* Translated and annotated by J. G. Pilkington. Edinburgh: T&T Clark, 1876.

———. *Expositions on the Book of Psalms by St. Augustine, Bishop of Hippo.* 6 vols. Oxford: John Henry Parker, 1853–1857.

Bach, Johann Sebastian. *St. Matthew Passion*. Translated by Helen Johnston. London: Bach Society, 1854.

Columba. "Prayer of St. Columba." In *Carmina Gadelica: Hymns and Incantations*, vol. 1. Translated by Alexander Carmichael. Edinburgh: Macleod, 1900.

Dostoyevsky, Fyodor. *The Brothers Karamazov*. Translated by Constance Garnett. London: Heinemann, 1912.

Epistle to Diognetus. In *The Apostolic Fathers, Justin Martyr, Irenaeus.* Vol. 1 of *The Ante-Nicene Fathers*, Series 1. Edited by Alexander Roberts and James Donaldson. New York: Scribner's Sons, 1903.

Hugo, Victor. *Les Miserables*. Translated by C. E. Wilbour. London: Chatto and Windus, 1874.

"Jesus soit en ma teste." In Old Sarum Primer and *Pynson's Horae*. London, 1514.

Luther, Martin. *What Luther Says: An Anthology*. Compiled by Ewald M. Plass. St. Louis: Concordia, 1959.

Martyrdom of Polycarp. In *The Apostolic Fathers*. Vol. 1 of *The Writings of the Apostolic Fathers*. Edited by Alexander Roberts and James Donaldson. Translated by Alexander Roberts, James Donaldson, and Frederick Crombie. Edinburgh: T&T Clark, 1870.

Polycarp of Smyrna. *The Apostolic Fathers*. Translated by J. B. Lightfoot. Edited by J. R. Harmer. London: Macmillan, 1898.

Theodoret of Cyrrhus. *The Ecclesiastical History, Dialogues, and Letters of Theodoret*. Translated by Blomfield Jackson. In vol. 3 of *The Nicence and Post-Nicene Fathers*, Series 1. Edited by Philip Schaff and Henry Wace. London: Parker & Co., 1892.